Proceeds

All proceeds from the sale of this book, after taxes and printing costs, will be donated to benefit the poor. For more information you may visit the web page: www.eaglenestpress.com/donation

About the Author

Mark Rais received a Master of Arts in Technical Writing and Editing from George Mason University, Virginia. He authored the Unix manual *The Essential Guide to OSF1*. During this time he also served as editor-in-chief of *Computer Reality Magazine*.

Mark's Linux operating system experience grew through the years he worked as Sr. Technical Manager at AOL Time Warner. A few of his professional Linux adventures include the creation of intranet tools for technology departments and management of the America Online, Inc. online publishing engineering teams.

When he's not busy installing Linux servers, Mark enjoys writing literary and non-fiction books.

Acknowledgements

There are so many people that helped make this book possible. But standing out are my special supporters and encouragers. My dear wife and greatest friend and my very special children who are the most wonderful gifts in life.

Most of all, I give credit to the one who gives lasting hope, Jesus Christ. Jesus took me from a broken life of sin and futility, and He gave me a full life and eternal hope. This came when I stopped trying to be good enough to get to God, but realized that God in love came instead to me. Jesus came not to condemn me but to save me through his sacrifice. By my simple belief in Him, I am able to be free from my fears and failures and to live a purpose-filled life that leads to heaven with Him.

I also want to thank my dad, mom, and sister who showed me a piece of this love God has for all of His creation.

What about Mohammed B., John N., Eric N., and other friends I've met over the years and learned from? I thank each of you for hanging in there through the annoying questions in my zeal to learn Linux in depth.

Finally, and with great gratitude I thank the many unnamed heroes who work day to day with Linux and truly prove that it can do marvelous things. Thank you!

Contents

continued...

SECTION 5: Appendix

SECTION 6: Total Index

Introduction
Another Linux Book?

Why in the world would someone take up the voluntary task of writing another Linux book? Could it be sheer lunacy? Maybe it's the result of monitor radiation?

Well, not really. The reason I chose to write this book was to resolve a nagging issue many have when starting out with Linux. We all need somewhere to go for those basic answers and tips without having to sift through intimidating and expensive 600 page manuals. How often the basic information we need is answered disjointedly on a dozen or so pages across several such manuals.

I spent countless and pain filled hours hunting through giant books, volumes of resources, and web page after web page as I was starting out with Linux. It was frustrating and often fruitless. I wanted one book to help me break into the Linux world with ease and enjoyment. The other manuals would then become far more relevant and useful.

Well, as my wife reminds me, don't complain so much about it or you'll end up doing it yourself. She was right as always, and here I am compiling the book whose various chapters and tips helped me personally break into the Linux world with fun rather than frustration.

I assure you this book doesn't answer every Linux question out there, nor does it include steps for every available Linux flavor.

Instead, what this book tries to address are the most common issues and the most basic steps we all face, but often have no one to ask. Included are beginner guides to Linux installation, configuration, and use.

The tips and steps in this book come out of real world experiences. Many pages are a result of documenting answers to questions so often asked by friends and colleagues who were getting started on the fascinating adventure of loading Linux.

I hope you'll find this book both useful and enjoyable!

Please Read This Page
Using This Book

To get the most out of this book you may want to review these basic conventions and design elements used throughout the chapters. When using the information in this book please keep the following in mind:

1. Tips

 Where you see the friendly little penguin you'll find a useful tip gained from personal experience. The penguin wants to help you avoid pain, so take a moment to read his suggestions.

2. Commands

Whenever you come across text that is in a strange `courier` font it is almost always a command that needs to be typed or text that will be displayed on the computer screen. As always, you must press the enter key to invoke any command.

3. The Prompt

Often, steps in this book refer to using the **command prompt**, an **xterm**, or your **terminal**. You can get to such a prompt by choosing from the main menu, within the *System Tools* folder, `terminal` or `xterm`. You may also find this by choosing *Run Program* and typing: `xterm`

4. Flavors

I've tried to keep most of the commands and steps in this book as generic as possible. However, in a few instances the examples given relate more closely to the Red Hat Linux flavor.

5. Troubleshooting

In many cases, I include **Troubleshooting** tips at the *end* of chapters where they are relevant. I've also included a basic question and answer appendix for broader topics.

Section 1
The Raw Basics

Chapter 1
Installing Linux Basics

This chapter is written to help those who need a simple installation guide with real world advice. Please always think before you do, since any installation will wipe out data on the installed partition.

Before You Begin
- If you are interested in simply creating a **Linux Boot Disk** then go to page 31, *Creating a Boot Disk*.
- If you just need advice on how to **configure your server** then move ahead to page 63, *Configuring a Linux Server*.
- If you have not yet finalized where you want to install Linux or which operating systems you want on the system, then please take a moment to read the *Dual Booting* recommendation on page 9.

Otherwise, read on for more detailed installation tips.

The following sections include the usual steps that will appear as your Linux installation progresses:

Starting the Installation
If you're not excited yet, you'll soon be as you slip your Linux CD-ROM into the drive and let the installation program start!

Sticking your Linux CD into the drive and rebooting your system should automatically start the installation.

If it does not, then you may need to change your system's BIOS settings to allow the CD-ROM drive to be the first drive to boot from. This is usually done by pressing the Delete key or F2 key when the system starts.

In some instances, you may instead need to create a boot disk to begin the installation. Go to page 31 if you need to make a boot disk.

Once the system boots from the Linux CD and the installation program begins, you can start using the steps on the following pages.

Basic Installation Setup

Almost all of the newer flavors of Linux begin with a very basic installation setup that allows you to choose your language, keyboard, and mouse settings. This is only for installation and won't affect your final setup.

Choose *Custom* Installation

Remember that all flavors of Linux are slightly different, but the essential steps are the same. In almost all cases you begin by having to choose from *workstation, server,* or *custom*. The latest Red Hat version also includes *Personal Desktop,* which is very basic and leaves out useful tools.

- **Custom** installation allows you to make changes as you go through the installation procedure. It gives you maximum flexibility.
- **Workstation** will simply leave off a lot of stuff you may want such as ftp, web server, telnet capability, etc.
- **Server** is a hard core installation that is strictly intended to give you a Linux server with high performance. In other words, using *Server* means there is very little else on the system except the core files.

I choose **Custom** all of the time, no matter who I'm installing for or what the purpose is, since it gives me the most control and flexibility.

Partitioning

Most flavors of Linux, including Mandrake, Red Hat, and Slackware, will give you the option of automatically partitioning or allowing you to custom partition.

⦿ Automatically partition
○ Manually partition with Disk Druid
○ Manually partition with fdisk

If you don't plan to do anything fancy with your server, then please choose Automatic partitioning (often called *Basic*). Using a newer version of Linux, the result will be a very simple partitioning of your hard disk into three sections. This is fine for basic work or beginner use.

However, I strongly prefer to use **Disk Druid** tool (often called *Expert*) to enhance my partitions and to give me more flexibility. (*see page 10*)

I rarely use fdisk, although with some flavors it is the only option. When I do use fdisk, it's only for cases that require complicated partitions.

If you choose **Automatic** (*Basic*) partitioning you will likely see:

Select the drive(s) to use for this installation:			
☐	hda	13037 MB	IBM-DJNA-371350
☑	hdb	8691 MB	WDC AC29100D

☑ Review (and modify if needed) the partitions created

It is absolutely **critical** that you **ONLY** select the hard disk/s that you want Linux running on! Otherwise, you will lose all data on all drives! In this example I've **unselected** my Windows hard drive (*hda*). Once you've chosen which drive to automatically partition, please skip ahead to page 12.

However, if you prefer to choose the **Disk Druid** tool (sometimes called *Expert*), please turn to the *next* page for details on partitioning.

Dual Booting?
How can I add partitions to the same hard disk on which I have Windows or another OS?

The short answer is that this *can* be done, but must be done carefully! The long and well documented answer is found best on your specific Linux flavor's website.

For me to write even some of the variations for dual boot machines would end up well beyond the scope of this basic book! I have to be open and tell you I can not recommend sharing the same hard drive between multiple Operating Systems, especially when new hard disks are so cheap. You'll also find that some operating systems make it very difficult to have a dual boot with Linux.

However, there are some options for sharing Linux and another OS:
1. Run Linux under another OS like MS Windows. This is not at all recommended since you will lose many of the benefits of Linux.
2. Erase all of the current partitions and make new ones to handle both Operating Systems. For instance you would create a vfat partition for Windows, and several ext3 partitions for Linux. This takes a lot of time, and requires a full reinstall. But it offers you a way to share *one* hard drive with several Operating Systems.
3. Purchase a second hard drive and install it into your system as the Linux hard drive. You can still choose which OS to load, but they are safely on separate hard drives in their own partitioning schemes.

NOTE that some versions of Windows have issues when placed on the 2nd drive. You may need to place Windows on the primary drive.

Using Disk Druid to Add Partitions

To add partitions (aka: Mount points) be certain the hard drive that is selected is really and truly the one you want Linux partitions on! All data on the selected partition will be deleted. (If you're installing Linux on a **non**-dual boot machine, this isn't an issue for you.)

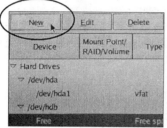

In this example, I press the *New* key (*Add* on some versions) to begin creating new mount points/partitions using Disk Druid.

If you are replacing an OS with Linux, then you may first need to *Delete* existing partitions of the hard drive.

Once you press *New* or *Add* to begin making mount points, you will see another window appear, usually labeled *Add Partition*. You may now begin adding the partitions you need for your server.

TIP: For *dual-boot* systems with more than one hard drive, please be certain that for each of the next few steps the *Allowable Drive* selected is **only** the one you want for deleting and creating Linux partitions on! You must do this each time you add a new partition mount point!

[ ] hda
[✓] hdb

A. Create Mount Point: /boot

Create Mount Point **/boot** which will be the area where Linux kernel and startup information is kept. I usually allocate several hundred MB at most to this. For this installation I assigned 133MB.

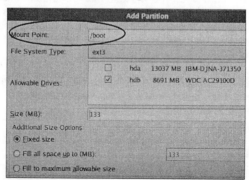

B. Create mount point: /

Create the Mount Point / that will be the area where root files and most programs are kept. I usually recommend at least having 2GB in this area.

C. Create mount point: <Linux Swap>

Create the Mount Point <Linux Swap> by going to the *Partition Type,* also called *File System Type,* and choosing Swap. Scroll down until you see Swap and select it. The Mount Point field will automatically fill in for you in most versions. The swap partition is a partition used to store temporary system data.

I usually make the swap file *smaller* than my total system RAM or the system will end up swapping more than storing in memory! For instance my server has 512 MB of RAM, and I create a Swap of 256 MB.

If you do this, on some of the newer versions of Red Hat and Mandrake you'll get a strange error complaining that the Swap file is too small. You can just ignore this message as long as you have made your swap size *larger* than 100 MB.

D. Create Mount Point: /usr

Create Mount Point **/usr** which is the area where user related programs and files go. Be sure to select the option for *Use Remaining Space.* In some flavors this option is called *Fill to maximum allowable size.*

This will correct the Actual size so that the remainder of your hard drive space is given to /usr. You should have at least 4GB of total disk space available to install everything from your Linux CD! For more information on package sizes, please read *Package Installation* on page 15.

TIPS: You can also add the **/home** mount point to ensure there is a unique mount point for individual users.

This is very helpful if you expect a lot of users on this server and intend to add additional disk drive space for them in the future.

Choosing Partitions to Format

Some of the newest versions of Linux **do not show** this step.

On some versions of Linux, you will see a **listing of the mount points** just created and their exact path name, including the specification of which hard disk they will be placed on. Remember hda is the master hard disk of your system. Don't allow formatting of this drive unless you are certain it is the one you want Linux placed on.

There's no need to check for Bad Blocks (an optional check box) unless you suspect your hard disk has errors.

Also, if you're using an older version that includes this step, you may also need to skip ahead briefly to *Creating a Boot Disk* on page 31.

Boot Loader Configuration

Use LiLo or GRUB as your default boot loader.

If LiLo is not the default for your Linux flavor you can select it by choosing to *Change the Boot Loader*. In some instances, a newer boot loader named GRUB is set as default. It's totally a matter of choice. I prefer to stick with LiLo since I've used it without issue for the last eight years. However, others prefer GRUB. Just make sure you choose a boot loader!

The boot loader must be placed on your first or master hard disk to work properly (*hda*).

If you are given the option of putting LiLo on the *MBR* (master boot record) **OR** on the *First Sector*, choose *MBR,* unless you plan on using a dual boot server with Windows NT.

Network Setup

Unselect the DHCP option and be sure to set a host name manually.
I usually set up stand-alone Linux servers, such as intra-office web servers. So in almost no case do I use DHCP (Dynamic Host Configuration Protocol). You can certainly use DHCP if you want another server to establish this system's network IP, but frankly this seems rather silly to me.

Hostname is usually a simple name such as: `myserver`

For some Linux versions, usually the simplified releases, the installation does not include steps to go through the details of network host and IP installation. In any case, I recommend that you add this information manually. You can always add or change network configurations later by typing at the Linux command prompt: `netconfig`

Manually insert the system's IP address and host name. You can do this in some Linux flavors by pressing the *Edit* button next to your Network Device name. Then unselect the DHCP option!

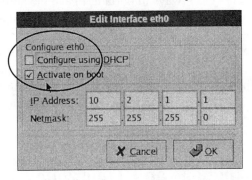

Let me give my own server IPs as an example. I'm running my server behind a firewall and simply need to designate this server's host name as myserver and IP as 10.2.1.1.

Just type in your machine's IP and netmask into the available fields.

Some releases of Mandrake, Red Hat, and Slackware, once you designate the IP, will automatically fill in fields like Netmask and Gateway. If your Linux fills in Netmask for you, please be sure you really should be using the default setting of 255.0.0.0! Most networks require 255.255.255.0.

The fields that will not be filled in are your DNS server IPs. You need to get them off another machine in your local network area or simply ignore them for now if you don't have a domain name server.

TIPS: In many cases the easiest way to figure out what all these numbers should be in a business setting is to check a PC nearby. To find out about your particular network's IP information you may try these:

- If you have other Linux servers already in your LAN then use the command: `netstat`
- If you have Windows systems in your LAN use the command: `winipcfg`

Firewall Settings

Just leave your firewall settings on **Medium** if you have no idea what to do! This should be fine for running something like a simple Linux intranet web server. At the same time, you need to consider the security risk of your particular system. If it's going to connect directly to the Internet the risk goes up substantially.

TIP: I am installing a server *within* the corporate firewall and although security is always important, I have the ability to simplify my life by customizing the Medium secure firewall by doing the following:

- Selecting ETH0 (my server's ethernet card) as a trusted device
- Selecting the TCP, FTP, SSH, and Telnet options to allow incoming access from these connections and applicable ports. This is **NOT** a good idea if your server is going to be connected to the internet!

Picking Language and Time zone

Just choose a language and move on!

TIP: Leave the language setting on *default* and move on to the next step! I had a colleague who thought it would be funny to try out a new and unique language for his Linux server. He chose something that basically made his server totally unreadable to him and required a complete reinstallation. I guess the joke was on him!

Time zones: It's important to choose the right time zone, since otherwise your users will be negatively affected. Users don't think it so funny if their files and all of their program date stamps are wrong by several hours! It's also important to set the server time correctly since there are many CRON or other time sensitive jobs that need accurate time settings!

Creating Root and New User

I can't stress enough to make the root password something simple to remember and *yet* hard to crack. More times than I prefer to count, I've had friends phone me late at night asking if I could help them recall the root password they created during our installation!

Full access login on any Linux server is *root* by default.

Also, take time to add an additional login account to your server. You may do this by pressing the *Add* button or the *new user* option.

Take time to create an additional user account for yourself. I always have a secondary login for my servers since I can do some things under root that are very dangerous! I usually create one other account for myself and continue on with the installation.

Password Protection

I always use **MD5** passwords and **Shadow** Passwords.

I rarely enable **NIS, LDAP, or Kerberos**. On the latest Red Hat and Mandrake releases, SMB is also an option. In some corporate situations where Kerberos IDs are standard I must include this. However, for a simple Linux server none of these are necessary.

Package Installation

Now when it comes time to select which Linux applications you want to install, there is a vast array of options! Many times, simply installing everything will work just fine! Do so if you have time and disk space!

What you personally decide to do is a matter of choice, but should be tempered with the fact that installing **everything** doesn't make life easier, but installing **too few** things will definitely make life harder!

 I strongly recommend you install **both** *KDE* and *GNOME* interfaces which come with their own distinct applications. These are two of the popular X-Windows Desktop interfaces.

It is well worth installing these two interface managers, even if you only plan on using one, since the installation will add lots of extra applications and goodies for you.

The choices are yours to make and I recommend you take time to read through the basic listing. If you plan to install everything, be sure you have allowed at least 4GB of space. By leaving off a number of the developers' tools like *Kernel Development* and some *Servers* I never use like DHCP and News servers, the installation takes around 2GB.

Also, since it's been a point of confusion to many, you don't need to install the *Windows File Server* to just do basic file sharing between your Linux machine. This server actually loads SAMBA and other tools.

Please note that some of the tools I refer to in this book are going to be installed **only** if you select the right packages or install everything.

Creating an Emergency Boot Disk

Some of the older versions of Linux include this step right after *Choosing Partitions to Format.* Others simply include this at the very end.

Now, is this a good idea? Well, yes! In fact, not creating a boot disk and simply skipping the option is as silly as throwing rocks at a hornet nest. You may get away with it for a while, but it'll sting you eventually!

You can create a boot disk **after installation** too, but it is not as easy. If you have already installed Linux but need a boot disk, then please see the chapter 6, *Creating a Boot Disk.* Otherwise, go ahead and let the installation make a boot disk for you.

That's It!

This takes care of most of the installation steps! Shortly, you'll have a Linux server of your very own installed and ready to run!

First Time Boot-Up Troubleshooting

The first time you start the Linux server, you'll notice a number of detailed configurations information scroll across your screen. Next to all of these should be a green check or the word OK. However, if you encounter issues, I list some suggestions below:

- If starting your system results in an indefinite hang at the initial load up, it may require turning off and back on your PC. If this doesn't fix it, you may have to try using your emergency boot disk. Sometimes this is a result of a serious error caused by a bad installation.
- Other symptoms of a bad install include Hard Disk errors that prompt you to use `fsck` to correct. These usually mean your hard drive has bad sectors, or that the Linux installation files were corrupted and require you to do a reinstall.
- If you get to the startup and next to Eth0 is the word Failed, you may need to simply plug in a LAN cable to your system's network card.

Chapter 2
Basic Linux Commands

I call these commands "basic" since they are the essential and core commands for people brand new to Linux.

Can you find a list like this somewhere else? Sure. However, what I've tried to do is weed out the hundreds of commands that I never use so only the most relevant things are listed for easy review.

All of these commands work from your command prompt. You must follow each command by pressing the enter key. The note "EX:" stands for example and is not part of the command. Also, please be aware that in Linux all commands are **case sensitive**!

You may hold down the Ctrl key and press c to stop (break) a command that is processing.

Use **cd** to change directories	Type **cd** followed by the name of a directory to move to that directory location. Ex:
	`cd games`
	If the directory *games* is not located hierarchically below the current directory, then the complete path must be written out. Ex:
	`cd /usr/games`
	To move up one directory, use the shortcut command. Ex:
	`cd ..`

Use **finger** to see who's on the system	Typing **finger** allows you to see who else is on the system or get detailed information about a person who has access to the system. Type **finger** followed by the name of a user's account to get information about that user. Or, type finger and press enter to see who's on the system and what they are doing. Ex: `finger johndoe`
Use **logout** to quit using the system	Yep, you guessed it, typing **logout** will log your account out of the system. Type logout at the prompt to disconnect from your Linux machine or to logout a particular user session from the system. Keep in mind that although rudimentary, leaving your critical account logged on may be a security concern. I recommend using logout when finished using your root account! Ex: `logout`

Basic Linux Commands continued...

Use **ls** to list files and directories
 	
Also use with the |**more** to allow scrolling.
	Type **ls** to see a list of the files and directories located in the current directory. If you're in the directory named *games* and you type **ls**, a list will appear that contains files in the games directory and sub-directories in the games directory. Examples:
	`ls Mail`
	`ls /usr/bin`
	Type ls -alt to see a list of all files (including .rc files) and all directories located in the current directory. The listing will include detailed, often useful information. Examples:
	`ls -alt`
	`ls -alt /usr/bin`
	
	If the screen flies by and you miss seeing a number of files, try using the | `more` at the end like:
	`ls -alt |more`
	
	If the `-alt` displays far too much detail for your liking, then trying using the command which lists all files without details:
	`ls -a`

Use **man** to pull up information about a command	Type **man** followed by a command to get detailed information about how to use the command. **Ex:**
	`man ls`
	Type `man -k` followed by a *word* to list all of the commands and descriptions that contain the word you specified. **Ex:**
	`man -k finger`

Use **more** to read the contents of a file	Type **more** followed by the name of a text file to read the file's contents. Why do I emphasize using this on a "text" file? Because most *other* types of files will look like garbage! **Ex:** `more testfile.txt`
Use **passwd** to change your current password	Type **passwd** and press enter. You'll see the message *Changing password* for *yourname*. At the `Old password:` prompt, type in your old password. Then, at the `Enter new password:` prompt, type in your new password. The system double checks your new password. Beside prompt `Verify:`, type the new password and press again. Create a secure password that combines parts of words and numbers. For instance, your dog's name may be Rufus. He may have been born in 1999. Create a password that uses **parts** of both the name and date of birth, such as '99rufu.

Use **print** to print a file	Type **print** *filename*. Obviously this assumes your Linux server has been setup to support your printer! Be sure to replace the word *filename* with a name of an actual text file. Printing the file doesn't take very long, so run over to the printer and see if it worked. **Some alternative options:** Want to print to a LAN printer? You'll have to refer to the network configuration section to make sure your Linux is ready for printing across the network. Of course, you could try and see what happens by holding shift and pressing Print Screen when viewing a file to see if it works. Want to print out on your own personal printer? Using the printscreen key or a screen capture command is a fast hack.
Use **pwd** to list the name of your current directory	Type **pwd** and hit enter. You'll see the **full** name of the directory you are currently in. This is your directory path and is very handy. This is especially handy when you forget which directory you've changed to and are trying to run other commands.

Chapter 3
Manipulating Files

This chapter is intended to help the beginner come up to speed on core file handling commands including file permissions. Included in this section are the commands needed to copy, delete, move, and rename files. File permissions are also reviewed below in the chmod command.

To see commands related to Directories rather than files, please skip ahead to page 25.

Are You a Beginner? It may help you to type the command `ls -alt` to list all of your current files and directories before you start, so you can see your directory and files listed.

Already have experience? Then please skip to page 27.

chmod	The **chmod** command allows you to alter access rights to files and directories. All files and directories have security permissions that grant the user particular groups' or all other users' access.

To view your files' settings, at the shell prompt type: `ls -alt`

You should see some files with the following in front of them (an example follows):
```
total 4
drwxrwsr-x 7 reallyli reallyli 1024 Apr 6 14:30 .
drwxr-s--x 22 reallyli reallyli 1024 Mar 30 18:20 ..
d-wx-wx-wx 3 reallyli reallyli 1024 Apr 6 14:30 content
drwxr-xr-x 2 reallyli reallyli 1024 Mar 25 20:43 files
```

What do the letters mean in front of the files/directories mean?
r indicates that it is readable (someone can view the file's contents)
w indicates that it is writable (someone can edit the file's contents)
x indicates that it is executable (someone can run the file, if executable)
- indicates that no permission to manipulate has been assigned

continued on the next page...

chmod	When listing your files, the first character lets you know whether you're looking at a file or a directory. The next three characters indicate **Your** access restrictions. The next three indicate your **group**'s permissions, and finally **other** users' permissions. Use **chmod** followed by the permission you are changing: chmod 755 *filename* The example above will grant you full rights, group rights to execute and read, and all others access to execute the file.

#	Permission
7	full
6	read and write
5	read and execute
4	read only
3	write and execute
2	write only
1	execute only
0	none

	Still confused? Use the table above to define the settings for the three "users." In the command, the first number refers to **your** permissions, the second refers to **group**, and the third refers to **general** users. Typing the command: chmod 751 *filename* gives **you** full access, the **group** read and execute, and **all** others execute only permission.
cp	To copy files. Type **cp** followed by the name of an existing file and the name of the new file. Ex: cp newfile newerfile To copy a file to a different directory (without changing the file's name), specify the directory instead of the new filename. Ex: cp newfile testdir To copy a file to a different directory and create a new file name, you need to specify a directory/a new file name. Ex: cp newfile testdir/newerfile cp newfile ../newerfile The .. is one directory up in hierarchy.

mv	To rename or move files from one directory to another. Type **mv** followed by the current name of a file and the new name of the file. Ex:
	 `mv oldfile newfile`
	
	 Type mv followed by the name of a file and the new directory where you'd like to place the file. Ex:
	 `mv newfile testdir`
	 This moves the file named newfile to an existing directory named testdir.
	 Be certain you're specifying a directory name or the mv command alters the name of the file *instead* of moving it.

rm	To remove or delete files. Type **rm** followed by the name of a file to remove the file. Ex:
	 `rm newfile`
	
	 Use the wildcard character to remove several files at once. Ex:
	 `rm n*`
	 This command removes all files beginning with n.
	
	 Type rm -i followed by a filename if you'd like to be prompted before the file is actually removed. Ex:
	 `rm -i newfile`
	 `rm -i n*`
	 By using this option, you have a chance to verify the removal of each file. The -i option is very handy when removing a number of files using the wildcard character *.

Chapter 4
Directory Commands

This chapter is intended to help novices easily learn the core directory commands for Linux .

If you're a beginner, it may help to type the command `ls -alt` to see a list of files and directories. Type this after trying *each* command to ensure it works properly. If you already have experience with directories and files, then skip to page 27.

cd	Use **cd** to change directories. Type cd followed by the name of a directory to access that directory. Keep in mind that you are always in a directory and can navigate to directories hierarchically above or below. Ex: `cd games` If the directory games is not located hierarchically below the current directory, then the complete path must be written out. Ex: cd /usr/games To move up one directory, use the shortcut command. Ex: cd ..
cp	Use **cp** -r to copy a directory and all of its contents Type cp -r followed by the name of an existing directory and the name of the new directory. Ex: `cp -r testing newdir` You must include the -r or you'll see the following message: cp: testing is a directory and -r not specified. This command saves you time if you need to make a mirror image of a directory packed with files.
mkdir	Use **mkdir** to make/create a brand new directory Type mkdir followed by the name of a directory. Ex: `mkdir testdir`

Directory Commands continued...

`mv`	Use **mv** to change the name of a directory Type mv followed by the current name of a directory and the new name of the directory. Ex: `mv testdir newnamedir`
`pwd`	Trying to find out where on your Linux server you currently are located? Are you confused what directory you are in? The **pwd** (print working directory) command will show you the full path to the directory you are currently in. This is very handy to use, especially when performing some of the other commands on this page!
`rmdir`	Use **rmdir** to remove an existing directory (assuming you have permissions set to allow this). Type rmdir followed by a directory's name to remove it. Ex: `rmdir testdir` You can't remove a directory that contains files. This command is used to remove *empty* directories. You'll need to delete or move the files before attempting to remove a full directory. See the **mv** command and also the previous chapter on *Manipulating Files*.

Chapter 5
Commands for Sharp Novices

A handful of friends kept demanding a single list of the most frequently used Linux commands. To keep my friendships in tact and because the idea seemed beneficial, I compiled these commands into a list for those ready to go to more advanced Linux use.

Now finally, we can all go to one place for commands we use so often, that provide more advanced functions we all need to reference.

du	The **du** command prints a summary of the amount of information you have stored in your directories on the mounted disks. syntax: du [options] path `ex: du -a /News` Options: -s print the sum of bytes in your directories -a print a line for each file in your directory
grep	The **grep** command searches text files for a particular *word* or *string* of words. It is very helpful when trying to find that needle in a haystack, like a particular line in a large log file. syntax: grep textstring filename(s) `ex: grep century history.txt`
Head & Tail	**head**: prints the beginning of a text file **tail**: prints the end of a text file These commands allow you to view parts of a text file. `ex: tail -5 textfile.txt` The example above will print the last 5 lines of the file textfile.txt.
Locate *Similar to* **which**	Trying to find out where on your Linux server a particular file resides? You can try using the `which` or `locate` commands to find the exact path to the file! Type: `locate` *filename* and press enter. Replace *filename* with the name of the file you are looking for. This is a real time saving command as you start navigating your Linux server! If locate does not work, try using the basic command: `which` Also, the 1st time you use locate type the command: **updatedb**

Commands continued...

Nice & Nohup	**Nice**: runs programs/commands at a lower system priority **Nohup**: runs nice programs even when you're logged off the system By using the *two commands* simultaneously, your large processes can continue to run, even when you have logged off the system and are relaxing. Ex: `nice nohup c program.c .` This command will allow the c compiler to compile program.c even when you have logged off the system.

ps related to "stopped jobs"	The **ps** command displays all of the existing processes. This command is also directly linked to issues with stopped processes (also known as "stopped jobs").
	
	Occasionally, you may see the message *There are Stopped Jobs.*
	
	If you log off the system without properly stopping your jobs, some jobs/processes may remain in memory tying up the system and drawing unnecessary processing bandwidth.
	
	Type `ps` and hit enter. This will list all of your current processes running, or stopped.
	
	The number under PID is the process identification number. To **kill** a process that is *stopped*, type: `kill pid`. Replace *pid* with the exact number of the process.
	
	`PID    TT STAT TIME  COMMAND`
	`23036 pl S    0:00  -csh`
	`23070 pl R    0:00  vi`
	
	Ex: While in Vi, you accidentally press the wrong keys. Vi's operation is stopped and you are kicked back to the prompt.
	To kill the stopped Vi command, you may type: `kill 23070`.
	
	These commands sound like something out of the dark ages, but are very easy to use once you know them.

`stty`	The **stty** command allows you to view a listing of your current terminal options. By using this command, you can also remap keyboard keys, tailoring to your needs. Ex: `stty` and hit enter. This lists your terminal settings. Ex: `stty erase\^h` This remaps your erase key (backspace) to the Ctrl and h keys. From now on, holding down Ctrl and pressing h will cause a backspace. So you're scratching your head asking why is this handy? You'll see at some point how stty is also used for a number of other useful settings. The most obvious benefit is to create short cuts and enhance your keyboard settings.
`talk`	In order to contact someone who is on the system, at the prompt you type: `talk accountname`. Replace *accountname* with the full account name of the person. If you don't want anyone to disturb you using the talk command, at the prompt type: `mesg n` This prevents others from using talk to reach you.
`tar` also related to gzip	You're bound to come across files that are **g-zipped and tarred**. Okay, now what? These are methods of compressing and storing directories and files in a single "file." Most new Linux programs come off the web named something similar to: coolnew-tool.4-4-01.gz. This file is likely a tar file that has then been gzipped for compression. The way to handle these files is simple, but requires that you put the file into an appropriate directory. In other words, don't plop the file in your root or /bin unless it belongs there. You can do a one fell swoop un-gzip and untar into its original form (usually multiple files in many sub directories) by typing: `tar -xvzf *.gz` This will automatically un-gzip and then untar all files in the current directory into their full original form including subdirectories etc. Please be careful where and how you run this!

Commands continued...

w	This command allows you to list all users and their processes currently running on your Linux server. It's extremely useful for system administration. Type: **w** to view all users' processes. Type: **w** jsmith to view jsmith's processes. I use this all the time from a system admin standpoint and also to figure out who I can use 'talk' with. It's a good idea to know who logs on to your system! Okay, so maybe you have a stand alone Linux box and no one else logs in to it? Try this command just to be sure. ;)
! !	Don't waste time and energy retyping commands at the prompt. Instead, use the ! option. To automatically re-display the last command you typed at the prompt, type: ! ! and press enter. Press again to invoke the command. You can also automatically re-display a command you typed earlier by using the ! and the first few letters of the command. Ex: At the Linux prompt you had typed the command *clear*, followed by the command *pico*, followed by the command *ftp*. In order to re-display the clear command you type: !cl and press enter. In order to re-display the last command you typed, simply type: ! ! Try it out. You'll find this a time saver when dealing with long commands, especially with long commands like tar! To go one further, you can also use the related command: history This lists *every* command you've used this session and lets you choose to reuse one from the list without retyping it! Try it by typing for example: history then typing: !32

Chapter 6
Creating a Boot Disk

*This short chapter was written to help those who **have already installed Linux**, but did not yet make an emergency boot disk.*

If you have **not yet** installed Linux and for some reason prefer to manually create a bootdisk rather than let the installation make it for you then please use the **rawrite** program included on your Linux CD-ROM, which is usually found under the *dosutils* subdirectory.

For general Linux Installation Help please go to the first chapter on *Linux Installation*.

Create An Emergency Boot Disk

1. Believe it or not you're going to need a *floppy disk* to do this so please make sure you have one handy!

2. Load up Linux and make sure you are logged in as *root* or have enough privileges to run system commands.

3. Check which Kernel you are running by typing exactly this at the command prompt:
`ls /lib/modules`

This should give you a directory item with the exact kernel such as: 2.4.2-2

4. Now insert your floppy diskette into the A: or floppy drive. In Linux the a: drive is also known as fd0 (that's with *zero* not an 'o')

5. At the prompt type: `mkbootdisk --device /dev/fd0 x.x.x-x` (replace the x.x.x-x with the kernel info you got from the step 3 above)

6. You should have an emergency boot disk within about 1 minute. All previous data on the floppy will obviously be erased.

7. Now you may use this floppy to boot in *emergency* situations!

On a final note for those with insatiable curiosity, when you use this Linux boot disk you will be overriding your existing LiLo boot-up loader on the hard disk. All this means is that you are exclusively booting from the floppy and no other options get loaded. However, you *can* make changes to which partition gets loaded with this boot disk by typing the change at the boot prompt such as: `/dev/hdb5`

 TIP: Don't get over happy with this floppy! There is almost NO real data on this emergency floppy boot disk. It is primarily intended to allow you to get access to the Linux partitions you may need to recover data from. It will NOT allow you to support a dual boot machine (ie. one where Windows is also available). You're only getting access to your Linux partitions for emergency fixes.

Troubleshooting Help
What if the `mkbootdisk` utility isn't available?

On some versions of Linux you can instead create a boot disk by typing this command at the Linux prompt:
`$ dd if=/mnt/cdrom/images/cdrom.img of=/dev/fd0`

Be sure that you have put your Linux CD into the CD-ROM drive and a floppy diskette into the floppy drive, and that **both** of these have been properly mounted (*see page 55*). Then run the command!

Section 2
Real World Use

Chapter 7
Vi, Pico, and Emacs

Text editors are similar to word processors, providing various features for editing files and writing documents. Several text editors are available for Linux, and this chapter explains how to use the three most popular.

Summary

Vi   (see page 36)

Vi is often the default editor that pops up on your Linux server when you're ready to write an e-mail message or when you're posting a News message.

Vi is sometimes seen as complicated and difficult to learn at first. However, because it is often the default editor for Unix and Linux systems, knowing how to use it is beneficial.

Pico   (see page 39)

Pico is a fairly simple text editor that provides straight-forward options and easy-to-use commands. On most of the newer Linux releases Pico does not come included by default.

Although some programmers have frowned at Pico's simplicity and limited options, many find that it provides everything necessary to write long documents with minimal hassles. However, Pico is problematic when manipulating certain types of files such as .cgi files.

Emacs   (see page 43)

Emacs falls somewhere between the straightforward Pico and the more complicated Vi. Unlike Vi, you don't need to switch between modes to perform basic text editing functions. Emacs is almost always available on your Linux system.

Sadly, the vast set of powerful commands themselves are difficult to remember and often remain unused features for day to day editing.

Vi Editor

Please skip past the brief Introduction below if you only need to see a list of commands for Vi use.

Introduction
Start the Vi editor by opening up an xterm window (when in Xwindows) or simply typing `vi` at the command prompt. Typing `vi` followed by a file name will automatically name the file so you don't have to worry about it later.

When you post to a News group or send e-mail, the system may default to Vi. How do you know when you're in Vi and when you can use Vi commands?

You're definitely in Vi when your system beeps at you and you see the following screen:

```
_
~
~
~
~
~
~
```

Vi has two modes:
- *Command* mode lets you use commands to edit, save, or quit
- *Text* mode lets you type and edit text

Use the **Esc** key to change from one mode to the other.

TIP: If you attempt to do something in the wrong mode, the system beeps furiously at you until you either stop pressing keys or scream (the louder the scream the more beeps you muffle).

Example of Using Vi:
1. Vi starts in the Command mode. To switch to text mode press i
2. Type out your text. To make corrections, move to a location in your text, or save your file, switch to the Command mode by pressing *Esc*.
3. In command mode you may edit, save, or exit (see Command Mode options on the next page for details).
4. To switch back to Text mode, type i again. Getting the hang of switching between modes may take a while, so please be patient with yourself.

Vi Text Writing Mode

The Vi editor starts in the Command mode. To switch to the Text mode and begin typing, press i. If you hear several beeps and you're unable to type, then press i twice to switch to the text mode.

Vi Command Mode

Press the Esc key to switch from Text mode to Command mode.

Moving Around (in the Command Mode):

To move	press
one character *left*	**h**
one character *right*	**l**
up one line	**k**
down one line	**j**

To	hold down
move *back* one screen	**Ctrl** and press **b**
move *forward* one screen	**Ctrl** and press **f**

In the Command mode you can also perform the important tasks of saving, exiting and editing your document. These options are listed in the next two tables.

Saving and Exiting (in the Command Mode)

To	type
quit Vi without saving anything (you'll lose any changes you made when using this command)	**:q!**
save/write the file you're working on without exiting	**:w** followed by *filename*
save/write your file and *quit* the vi editor in one step	**:wq**

Editing   (in the Text Mode)

To	hold down the **Ctrl** key and press	instead of
delete a character	**backspace**	backspace
move *up* a line	**p**	up arrow
move *down* a line	**n**	down arrow
move *left* one space	**b**	left arrow
move *right* one space	**f**	right arrow
move to the *end* of a line	**e**	End

To	type
cut a *character* directly above the cursor.	**x**
cut the entire *line* directly above the cursor.	**dd**
paste the last character or line that you cut on the line directly *below* the cursor.	**p**
paste the last character or line that you cut on the line directly *above* the cursor.	**P**
search forward through the document for specific text you designate. If Vi can not find the text, the message *Pattern not found* appears. Ex: /text string	**/**
search for the *same* text again (saves from retyping your search)	**n**
search backward through the document for specific text you designate. If Vi can not find the text the message *Pattern not found* appears. Ex: ?text string	**?**

Vi Troubleshooting Quick Tips
Command Mode Problems
- If you're trying to use a Move, Save, or Edit command, but the command isn't working, try pressing the **Esc** key.
- If the backspace key doesn't work, then hold down the Ctrl key and press backspace.

Problems Trying to Save in Vi
- If you get the message "No current filename," then in the Command mode type : w followed by a filename. This message appears only if a filename has not been specified.
- If you get the message "Is a directory," you may be trying to write to a directory name instead of a file. Use a different file name.

Pico Editor

Skip the introduction if you just need to see a list of commands under:
"Commands" and "Smorgasbord of Pico Options" on the next page.

Introduction

Start the Pico editor by typing `pico` at the command prompt. Note that some of the newer Linux flavors **do not** preinstall Pico for you.
Typing `pico` followed by a file name automatically names the file so you don't have to worry about it later. Example: `pico newfile.txt`

Using Pico is fairly straight-forward. Simply edit or type your text.
When you're finished typing, or anytime you're ready to use a Pico command, refer to the Pico menu options, listed at the bottom of the screen.

TIPS: Pico has a way of adding characters to ends of lines for you! Be careful, especially when editing server files like CGIs! I really recommend using a *different* editor to do complex editing work!

To use any Pico menu option, hold down the **Ctrl** key and press the letter of the option. On the menu the ^ symbol represents the Ctrl key.

Always refer to the bottom two lines of Pico to see what options are available to you. Depending on what you're doing in Pico, your options change.

Editing text

You can edit your document by using the arrow keys and the backspace key on your keyboard. Yep, it's that easy. No, the interface is not a real GUI, but it is far simpler than some of the other editors. On the next page you'll find lots of commands and options.

Commands

Depending on your Linux settings, the arrow keys or the backspace key may not work. Hopefully this is not the case. However if you're in Pico and need a quick solution to this you can use the commands listed on the next page to perform the same tasks. They're also great as shortcuts!

Smorgasbord of Pico Options

^C Cancel allows you to stop a process at any time. If you make a mistake in selecting an option, just hold down the **Ctrl** key and press **c**.

^G Get Help

Get clear and concise assistance from the Pico help, in case something unexpected happens or you need additional information about a command.

^X Exit

Exit Pico at anytime. If you've made changes to a file or you've worked on a new file, but you haven't saved the changes, you see this message: *Save modified buffer (ANSWERING "No" WILL DESTROY CHANGES) (y/n)?*
Answering no (press **n**) will close Pico and bring you back to the prompt without saving your file.
Answering yes (press **y**) will allow you to save the file you've been working on (see WriteOut section below for details).

^O WriteOut

Save your file without hassles or worries. Fill in the name of your file beside the File Name to *write:* prompt. If your file already has a name, then press enter.

^T To Files option lets you save your text over a file that exists in your directory. Pico takes you to a directory Browser.
Browser Options
To alter a file or directory, first use the arrow keys or the optional *movement* keys (described earlier) to highlight a particular name. You can also press **w** to find and highlight a file or directory quickly. Once you've highlighted a particular file or directory, you can use any one of these options.

> Type **e** to Exit the Browser
> Type **r** to rename a directory or file
> Type **d** to delete a file
> Type **m** to create an additional copy of a file
> Type **g** to move to another directory where the file is located
> Type **s** or press enter to write over the file with text you just
> > wrote in Pico

---

^R Read File
Insert text from another file into your current text file. This option allows you to search through your directories for a file that you would like to add to your text.

This option is especially handy if you've saved a document and would like to add its content to the new file you're working on. Text from the file you select is placed on the line directly above your cursor.

At the *Insert file:* prompt you may either type a file name or use the *Browser* options. You can use the same options as listed above under ^T.

^Y Prev Pg
Move quickly to the previous page. Although you could just as easily press the up arrow key several times, this command quickly jumps your cursor up one page.

^V Next Pg
Move quickly to the next page. Although you could just as easily press the down arrow key several times, this command quickly jumps your cursor down one page.

^K Cut Text
This option allows you to cut a full line of text. By using the *uncut* command and your arrow keys, you can then paste the cut text at another location in your document.

To cut text in a line or to cut several lines of text:
- Move the cursor to the beginning of the text you want to select
- Hold down the **Ctrl** key and press ^
- Use the right arrow key or hold down **Ctrl** and press **f** to highlight text
- When you have highlighted the appropriate text, hold down the **Ctrl** key and press **k** to cut it.
- Paste the text you cut, anywhere in your document, using UnCut Text

^U UnCut Text
Paste text that you previously cut. You can use this option to undo an accidental cut of text or place cut text at another location in your document. The text you cut is pasted on the line directly above your cursor.

Pico Commands Continued...
^C Cur Pos
Indicate the current position of your cursor, relative to the entire document. This is a helpful option if you'd like to check exactly where in your document you are. The status line indicates the following items:
```
[ line 8 of 18 (44%), character 109 of 254 (42%) ]
```

^J Justify
Even out lines of text. This command is handy when you accidentally type extra spaces between words or press the *enter* key before reaching the end of a line. The option evens the length of your text lines automatically.

^U UnJustify
UnJustify lines of text. For the messy line look you can always select the UnJustify option.

^W Where is
Find a particular string of text quickly. This option allows you to do a word search in your text. This option is especially handy for longer documents. If the word you designated at the *Search*: prompt is found, it places the cursor beside it.

^T To Spell
Check for spelling errors. If spell checker finds a misspelled word or a word it doesn't recognize (don't worry, this rarely happens), it will let you correct the word. At the *Edit a replacement:* prompt, type in the correct spelling of a word. However, if you don't want to make any changes, simply press the enter key.

Any words that you've corrected but re-occur in the document can be automatically replaced. At the *Replace a with b? [y]:* prompt press **y** to replace all occurrences of the misspelled word or **n** to ignore.

Emacs Editor

Skip ahead if you simply need to see a list of commands shown on the next page under "Commands."

Introduction
Start the Emacs text editor by typing emacs followed by a file name to name the file you plan on working on. You can also type the name of an existing file you want to edit.

TIPS: Emacs doesn't require you to switch between modes like Vi. However, when using Emacs, keep in mind these things:
- Sometimes you may need to press enter before reaching the end of a line
- All of the commands require you to hold down the Ctrl key and press a letter
- Messages that appear are usually loaded with jargon, so if you don't understand them, it's okay to ignore them.

Simple Example of Using Emacs:
- At the prompt type: emacs
  You may see a long and dull message appear on your screen.
- Start typing your document.
  To save your file, hold down the **Ctrl** key and press x, then hold down the Ctrl key and press w.
- Beside the prompt labeled Write file: ~/ type the name of your file and press enter.
  Example: Write file: ~/testfile.txt
- To quit Emacs, hold down the Ctrl key and press x then hold down the Ctrl key and press c

Please turn the page to review the most frequently used Emacs Commands listed for you in three basic tables.

Moving

To move	hold down the **Ctrl** key and press
back one character	**b**
forward one character	**f**
up one line (to the previous line)	**p**
down one line (to the next line)	**n**
the *end* of a line	**e**
the *start* of a line	**a**
down to the *next* screen	**v**

To move	hold down the **Esc** key and press
up to the *previous* screen	**v**
to the *beginning* of the file	**,**
to the *end* of the file	**.**

Editing

Using the movement keys, locate your cursor in the appropriate spot for editing. Besides using the *Delete* key to delete individual characters, you can use the following editing commands:

To	hold down the **Ctrl** key and press
delete a character to the left of the cursor	**backspace**
cut all text on a line to the *right* of the cursor	**k**
paste all text that was cut last	**y**
search forward for a text string	**s**
search backward for a text string	**r**
search for specific text in your file if the other search commands don't work	**>** , then hold down **Ctrl** and press **r**

Saving and Exiting

To	hold down the Ctrl key and
save your file	press **x**, then hold down the **Ctrl** key and press **w** type the name of the file beside the *Write file: ~/* prompt and press enter.
exit Emacs	be sure you've saved the changes you've made, then press **x**, now hold down the **Ctrl** key and press **c**

Emacs Troubleshooting Basics
Starting Emacs
You see a strange message such as:
```
;; This buffer is for notes you don't want to save...
```
Emacs requires a file name. If you're editing a new file you must name it before you can start working on it.

It's easy to resolve. At this point press the following:
- Hold down the Ctrl key and press x
- Now hold down the Ctrl key and press f
- At the prompt you should see `Find file:~/` At this prompt type the *name* of your new file you're creating and press enter.

Trying to Search
- If there are no other text strings that match the one you've searched for, you see the message: `Failing I-search backward:`
- Re-start your search or stop searching.

Trying to Save
- If you try to save a file that has the same name as a directory, you see the message: File `/home/mark/test` is a directory.
- You have to give your file a different name.

Chapter 8
X-Windows Tips for Newbies

Having spent a lot of late nights scratching my head trying to make X-Windows work smoothly on various PCs, I wanted to include some tips to help you avoid potential frustration.

For clarity I've broken this chapter into three subsections:
- Installation Tips and Traps
- Using X-Windows Tips
- Configuration Recommendations

Installation Tips and Traps
Know Your System
I guess this subheading should really be "Know your monitor and video card before installing!" Let's face it, for a smooth installation and use of X-Windows, you will need to know at least the basic specification of your monitor and video card or you may end up wasting a lot of time.

Right now, when you may still have Windows installed or easy access to the hardware manuals, go and check out exactly what the video card and monitor specs are. Don't wait! Save yourself! Please pause in reading this and do it!

BIOS Settings May Help
Okay, if you don't have the option of checking your exact monitor and video card specifications, and you're still having problems with installing X-Windows, then change your BIOS settings.

One big step that may help you is to restart your computer and change a BIOS setting before reinstalling.

On most systems you may press the *Delete* key or the F2 key to enter your BIOS setup features. This may be different for your PC and you'll need to verify with the manufacturer's documents. Once you're in the BIOS setup, look for something labeled *Plug&Play, PNP,* or *Plug'n'Play.*

The setting usually offers two options, either *software,* or *hardware.* On some computers the two options may be named *OS* and *System.* Now set your Plug'n'Play BIOS option to allow your **system** to configure the setting rather than the OS for better results when installing or configuring X-Windows.

If this entire section only confused you more, please forgive me and move on to the next section!

Avoiding Video Issues

One reasonable means of avoiding video problems is to choose fairly generic options such as video setting of 800x600 pixels, with vertical and horizontal rates around 31 to 50 range. You can also choose SVGA as the most generic monitor type.

Now, this is useful **only** IF the installation did not properly recognize your video card or monitor setting and you can't find your hardware **manually** from the list.

Using X-Windows Tips

How to Start X-Windows?

The easiest way to start up your X-Windows is to type at your command prompt: `startx`

How to Exit?!

One of the most common questions people ask me about X-Windows is how in the heck you can exit it if a problem arises!

To get the heck out of X-Windows, press these **3 keys** simultaneously: `Ctrl Alt Backspace`
In *some* cases you may need to press these keys twice!

How To Change Desktop GUIs?

Most versions of Linux come with several available Desktop GUIs that work in X-Windows. The Desktop (also called Window Manager) is the tool that controls your fancy icons, the way screens appear on the monitor, etc. As mentioned in chapter 1, Gnome and KDE are two of the most popular available desktops.

On all versions of Linux the ability to change your desktop is available at the Login prompt (graphical login where you type your name and password) or located under the current Desktop main menu as a menu item.

However, I've included a few additional flavor specific examples below:

- **Mandrake** allows you to change desktops with the `Boot Config` tool. It's usually available as a standard icon on your desktop.
- **Red Hat** versions also allow a very easy way to switch desktops by typing at the command xterm prompt: `switchdesk` If you're using a new version of Red Hat also try the command: `kpersonalizer`
- **Slackware** provides the standard *X Windows Manager* tool. You can use this when in X Windows by typing at the prompt: `xwmconfig`

Configuration Recommendations

Help -- X Still Doesn't Work Right!
On occasion, using X for the first time is like having your nails trimmed with a machinegun; it's going to hurt, and it'll cost you some blood! This is often the case when using very old or the very newest PCs that have unknown video drivers and monitors.

If your particular hardware profiles are not available during X Windows installation, the best bet is to get in touch with your specific flavor's technical help and ask them where to download the needed drivers or visit their specific website.

No matter what version you're using, these tips may help guide you to some answers.

A Few Top Troubleshooting Tips:

- Again, to get the heck out of X-Windows press these **3** keys simultaneously: **Ctrl Alt Backspace**
- Remember that in Linux, you can find files you're looking for by using the `locate` command. This is a BIG help for identifying where a certain file or directory is located on your system.
- Some X-Windows tools that you should be aware of and may use to help with configuration:
  `Xconfigurator` = configure X manually with this command
  `/usr/X11R6/bin/XF86Setup` = another config tool for X
  `SuperProbe` = video clock probing utility
  `redhat-config-xfree86` = configure X on *RedHat* versions

Stupidly Low Resolution

Okay, so you run `startx` and end up with a really pathetic screen resolution, like 320x200 pixels! Icons are as big as your monitor and you can't seem to change the resolution no matter how hard you try!!! Arggg! Yes, I've been there. I share your pain!

For many distributions it is best to first try using the Xconfigurator tool mentioned earlier. If this fails to help, then go to your flavor's website and try a search on something like *"X-Windows video configuration."*

TIP: The most popular flavors of Linux regularly update files that correct errors with video settings and place these files on their FTP sites. You may try looking into your flavor's FTP site.

Example FTP Site Use
Fixing Video Issues for *Some Red Hat* Versions

To correct some of the issues with video settings you may use these tips:
1. FTP to the mirror site for Redhat at:
   sunsite.ualberta.ca /pub/Mirror/Linux/redhat
2. Go to the `Updates` X directory (replacing X with which ever version you are using) and download the following files:
   ```
   XFree86
   XFree86-100dpi-fonts
   XFree86-75dpi-fonts
   XFree86-cyrillic-fonts
   XFree86-SVGA
   XFree86-VGA16
   XFree86-libs
   XFree86-xfsrpm
   ```

These files are all going to have the .rpm (RedHat Package Manager) extension and will *also include* your specific version numbers in the names!

3. Download the files and place them under any directory as long as you're logged in to Linux as *root*!
4. Next, run the rpm command below:
   ```
   rpm -uvh filename
   ```
   (replacing the word *filename* with a specific .rpm file)
5. Then reboot, and type the command: `Xconfigurator` to reset the resolution options for a *generic* video card. If you're using a new version of Red Hat type the command: `redhat-config-xfree86`

Let's face it, if we were using known name brand hardware or the latest Red Hat version, this would probably not be necessary! I think I'll upgrade!

Chapter 9
Accessing Windows Files
from Linux

This chapter is intended specifically for those with dual boot systems where Linux and Windows are available.

By taking the steps in this chapter you gain flexibility and ease of use for your Linux server, allowing you to easily exchange files with your Windows partition or drive.

Before you can Use it, Mount It

When you install Linux on a system with an existing operating system like Microsoft Windows it is easy to make those files and directories available under Linux.

Often newer installations of Linux even auto-mount certain things like floppy drives and CD-ROMs for you. However, it's common for your Windows disk/partition not to be automatically mounted for use.

To get access to your Windows drive/partition under Linux you may need to perform these simple steps:

1) Create a directory under Linux that will link to your Windows drive/partition at the prompt type: **mkdir /mnt/win**

2) Then mount your Windows drive and link it to this new directory under Linux at the prompt type exactly:
mount -t vfat /dev/hda1 /mnt/win

3) Now try changing directories to your Windows drive/partition by typing at the prompt: **cd /mnt/win** and then typing: **ls -all**

Notice that the actual disk or partition information in this example is /dev/hda1. This is *usually* the case if you have installed Linux onto a system with existing Windows.

The *hda1* refers to the first partition of your master (1st) hard drive.

However, in some cases you may be using a system where Linux is on the *hda1* and your Windows drive is actually something different. You will need to adjust based on what your Windows drive is.

If you have an error, check what drives and partitions are *already* mounted by simply typing the command: **mount**

To Use It, Navigate Directories

Once you've successfully mounted your Windows partition or drive so Linux can read it, you're ready to save and read files.

You may use your favorite Linux file manager or simply traverse the Windows files you need by using any Linux program. Any Linux program can save to the Windows partition or drive by using the *save as* feature and then navigating down the following Linux directories:
1. Go to the Linux /mnt/win directory (all drives are under /mnt)
2. Entering this will present you with your Windows directories
3. Save the file anywhere on the Windows drive you wish

Fast Way To Mount It

If you're planning to use the Mount command on the previous page regularly, you can simplify your life using a simple trick which works on just about every Linux version and flavor.

1. Save the mount command in a file using a text editor like Vi, Pico, or Emacs (see chapter 7). Do this by creating a file named winmount
2. In this file just add a line with the mount command:
    mount -t vfat /dev/hda1 /mnt/win
3. Save this file. Be sure you've already created the directory as mentioned on the previous page!
4. Now, whenever you need to run the mount command, simply type at your command prompt: bash winmount

Chapter 10
Dual Boot Settings

This chapter reviews how to change the actual boot up settings for dual boot machines. The information is provided for those who have already installed Linux on to a dual booting machine!

I try to provide a very simple overview of how to ensure your dual boot is set to load Linux or another OS as default, followed by tips for setting the length of time for the dual boot sequence.

PLEASE STOP and review *Boot loader Configuration* on page 12 if you have forgotten what these are: *boot loader, LiLo,* or *GRUB*!

Dual Booting Default

When you install Linux on a system with an existing operating system like Microsoft Windows you may want a way to customize how the dual boot options work.

To change which OS boots by default you may use the Linux configuration tool. At the command prompt just type: `Linuxconf`

*If this doesn't work, please take a look at the TIP on this page and the next page. For Mandrake users the tool is called **Boot Config**.*

In the tool Linuxconf, you will find a menu item labeled "boot mode" and then a tool called LiLo. Assuming your boot loader is LiLo, under the item "default boot configuration" simply select whichever OS you want to enable as default. Linux is usually the preset default.

 TIP: What if you can't find **Linuxconf** anywhere on your system? Chances are that when you installed Linux you may not have installed the specific package that it comes in. You can always download the tool from the web, although this is a lot more painful, by going to the site:
`http://www.solucorp.qc.ca/linuxconf/`

Dual Booting Time Limit

Often the system startup menu flies by so fast I can't switch the OS in time! This is due to the default time limit being far too short! In almost every case, when I install Linux on a dual booting machine, I need to change this setting to give me more time. Changing the time limit (time delay) is very helpful if you switch between Operating Systems frequently.

To change the delay time or time limit of your Dual Boot menu, find the System utility called *Linuxconf* usually found under your Main Menu. If you have a hard time finding it, try typing at the prompt: `Linuxconf`

Under Linuxconf, find a menu item labeled "boot mode" and then a tool called Lilo. Obviously, this applies **only** to LiLo boot loaded systems. Under the item "LILO defaults" look at the option for "Prompt time out"

in seconds. This is where you would type in how many seconds you want the system to wait for you to select an OS.

I've tried to depict this in the example illustration:

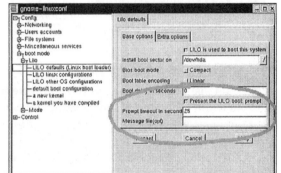

TIP: At least one new version of Linux stopped including the Linuxconf tool (which makes no sense to me whatsoever)! If you have a hard time finding this tool, and don't want to download it from the site mentioned on page 53, then instead you can edit the actual configuration files. Be very careful and make a backup!

If your system's boot loader is **LiLo**, then your configuration file is: `/etc/lilo.conf`
Change the line `timeout=x` where x is the number of milliseconds
Change the line `default=y` where y is usually either dos or linux
Save the file and run the command: `lilo -v -v`

If your system's boot loader is **GRUB**, then your file is: `/etc/grub.conf` (some Red Hat versions it's /boot/grub/grub.conf)
Change the line `timeout=x` where x is the number of seconds
Change the line `default=y` where y is usually either dos or linux

Chapter 11
Using Your Floppy Drive, Zip, or CD-ROM in Linux

I briefly mentioned the Mount command in the previous chapter on Accessing Windows Files. Now I want to include some details about mount and unmount when getting ready to use things like your floppy drive, or when shutting down your system.

In most cases your Linux flavor will already mount things for you without any issue. In fact, KDE Desktop interface comes with the handy little icons that auto-mount things like your floppy disk. Just click on them!

However, sometimes you may need or want the control yourself.

How to Mount Drives like a CD-ROM (mount)

The Linux server you installed may or may not have auto installed the mounts needed for using your cd-rom, zip drive, CD-R, DVD, or possibly even your floppy drive. Below are some sample steps to get a CD-ROM drive to mount. These same steps apply to most drives needing mount.

- Open an xterm session
- Find out what is already mounted by typing the command:
  `mount |more`
- Mount your CD-ROM, type the command:
  `mount /dev/cdrom`
  (mount a floppy instead with: `mount /dev/floppy`)
- The system will mount the drive and give a response
- Now you can begin using the CD-ROM by changing directories to the drive (likely): `cd /mnt/cdrom`
- Type: `ls -alt` to see if you mounted CD-ROM successfully

Run into a problem?
If you get an error:
"No medium found" you need to put in the CD into the CD-ROM drive or it can not mount. Same goes for floppy, or zip drive!

What if you get "No such file or directory"?

It is likely a problem with how you are trying to assign the name or path to your drive. For instance, floppy is often called fd0 not *floppy*. If this doesn't help, then try viewing the content of your fstab file. Do this:

- Type: `locate fstab`
- If this doesn't find the fstab location, try `cd /etc/fstab`
- **View** the content of fstab by typing: `more fstab` or using your favorite editor (don't edit it!)
- This should tell you the exact name and path of your drive, for example: `cd-rom /mnt/cdrom`
- Now you can go back to the previous mount instructions and use **this** path and drive

Turning Off a Server (unmount)

When you install Linux with all of those fancy and very powerful programs and utilities like NFS, Apache, etc., you're really starting a very complex and powerful server. Complete with security, file handling, web serving, and even remote dialup capabilities, your Linux box is equivalent to the computers NASA used to launch the space shuttle in the '80s! That's POWER!

But, with power comes the need for responsible use. Before you turn off the server, to avoid file system issues, you may want to use the following steps:

- In an xterm or at the prompt type the command: `umount -a`
- System will unmount all appropriate disks and alert you
- Now type the command: `shutdown now`
- System should tell you it is switching to single user mode
- Once in single user mode you can turn the server power off

Thankfully, these exact same steps are now done automatically for you on **some** of the latest versions of Linux when you press the reset button.

If you run into a snag, it may be that a device is busy and can not be unmounted. For instance, a CD-ROM drive may still be mounted. You need to make sure you're not using this drive (have an xterm open to cdrom etc.)! You can also type `mount` at the prompt to see what is actually mounted and in use.

Chapter 12
Running Windows Programs
from Linux

*For those with dual boot systems, I've included this section to show you a
way to run a few of your basic Windows programs from Linux.*

I need to be candid upfront and tell you that the WINE project has not yet
completed their mission of enabling a full emulation of Windows. However, I've gotten a number of Windows98 and Windows2000 programs
working with the WINE emulator.

Free Emulator Called WINE
WINE is available for free download from the project website you can
access at http://www.wine.org/. It also comes preloaded on most Linux
distribution CDs. You need to have the three core files for running
WINE properly: winerpm, an updated wine.conf, and user.dat. Most new
Linux versions come with these files, or you can download them from the
internet. The key is to have an *updated* wine.conf file which I describe
on the next page.

A lot of work and many hours of effort have paid off, and Linux users
actually can download and install a free emulator that runs many programs without any issue under Linux.

This does **not** mean that you will be able to run all of your software on
Linux. Nor does it imply that you do not need Windows98 or other Windows installed! You will need Windows installed on the same machine
as WINE, otherwise there is no way to "install" your Windows software
to run it in the first place.

OK, this may negate your reason for trying WINE, but I want to be
straight up before you begin this. Also, WINE does not support DOS
programs right now.

An old Linux emulator called *dosemu* had done this with some success.
Currently WINE is tuned for Windows98 programs. Sadly, this means a

lot of my old, still fun and paid for DOS games won't run under Linux! Okay, I admit that to some folks this is no loss.

Using WINE to Run Windows Programs
If you've followed the very first step mentioned earlier and downloaded and installed WINE on your Linux machine, then you are ready to try running your Windows program!

1   Check to see that the WINE program is truly installed by typing the command: `locate wine` You should see a list of files with the word WINE in them.

2   Be sure you have properly mounted your Windows drive. If you don't know how then read page 51 for details.

3   Edit the file `/etc/wine.conf` by changing the line with the text **[Drive C]** to read exactly: `Path=/mnt/win`

4   Save the edited wine.conf file and then make sure you also **copy** the file user.dat to your Windows directory, which is usually: `c:/windows/profiles/`

5   If you plan on running a game or other program that uses your midi then Linux midi-sequencer needs to be installed.

6   Now type this command paying attention to caps etc.:
`cd "/mnt/win/Program Files/Accessories"`
then type this: `wine ./calc.exe`

7   This will run Windows Calculator on your Linux! You can load any other programs by using *similar* commands, ***adjusting*** for directory names and file names as needed.

Troubleshooting and Tips
First of all disregard all of the detailed error information that may be displayed while you run Wine. Only on occasion do these error messages help you troubleshoot why a program does not run under WINE.

Second, many programs will not run properly under WINE unless your LINUX has been configured for sound and graphics. There are lots of details to this that I can't explain briefly here. You can refer to your specific Linux versions web site for details on configuring your sound and midi.

Finally, remember that you need to type the commands exactly as they appear, for instance when using long directory names you need to include the begin and end quote (") marks. When you try to run a program you should include the leading `./` in front of the executable program name as well.

WINE Doesn't Run What You Need
As always, you get what you pay for!

In the case of WINE you get a very good, simple emulator for free.

No, sorry it won't be able to run your latest version of Microsoft Office XP! For truly compatible Windows Office like programs see my chapter on *Dumping MS-Office for Linux StarOffice* on page 85.

If you're looking for commercial software that allows running most Windows programs under Linux then I highly recommend you check out two sites, the VMWare website http://www.vmware.com and also the program called Win4Lin at http://www.win4lin.com.

These companies have made a lot of progress for folks who are willing to pay some money to get the total flexibility of running both Linux and Windows on the same machine.

Section 3
Server Setup

Chapter 13
Configuring a Linux Server:
Httpd, MySQL, Telnet, FTP

This chapter includes details on how to configure Linux so that it will run your webserver, telnet, ftp, mysql and much more. I use this chapter to help remind myself of all the nuances and settings for servers I'm often installing late at night!

NOTICE: To change configurations and use these commands, it is essential that you are logged in to your Linux server as **root**, or have full super user access. If you're not you'll end up with a lot of strange errors like "file is not readable!"

For those who can not wait to read through the entire chapter, please look for a super fast review of the commands in the chart below.

Summary of Commands

Trying to Start:	Then Type This:
httpd	cd /etc/rc.d/init.d/ then type: ./httpd start
mysql	cd /etc/rc.d/init.d/ then type: ./mysqld start

telnet	Edit the file /etc/xinetd.d/telnetd
	changing the two lines to:
	# default: on
	disabled = no
	then run the command
	/etc/rc.d/init.d/xinetd restart

ftp	Edit the file /etc/xinetd.d/wu-ftpd
	changing the two lines to:
	# default: on
	disabled = no
	then run the command
	/etc/rc.d/init.d/xinetd restart

Configuring Your Linux Server

I should mention that this guide is best used when in front of your Linux box, with an open terminal (command prompt). The exact commands apply to most any Linux server, and I've included additional information when there is an obvious difference between some flavors.

Hopefully, after reviewing this chapter and using these steps, you'll enjoy the power of owning a full fledged Web, FTP, and DataBase server!

TIP 1: When you need to find a particular file or directory, use the 'locate' command to identify their exact path. For example, try typing the command: `locate httpd`

TIP 2: In case you were not aware, all of the web server files for many of the popular Linux versions are under: `/var/www`

Okay, let's get started configuring our server! The first step is to take stock of the system's current status and configuration.

Step 1. Which Processes are Running ?

If you don't know which processes are already active on your server, then you need to find out asap! Use this command at the prompt:
`/sbin/chkconfig --list`

The output will resemble something like this:

```
...
httpd 0:off 1:off 2:off 3:off 4:off 5:off 6:off
telnet :off
...
```

The command above will give you a long list of processes with info beside them like `off` or `on`. Any process with the word `off` next to it can be assumed *disabled* by default during startup.

You should look for your processes that are needed for running a server like: httpd, telnet, wu-ftp, mysqld. All of these should be `on` by default.

Step 2. Get Processes Started

Starting up your webserver (httpd), mysql (mysqld), sendmail, etc. is easy so long as you follow the directions from the steps below.

Your **webserver** and **mysql** can be enabled right away for use.

1st. Change to the initialization (aka. *init*) directory:
```
cd /etc/rc.d/init.d/
```

This directory (when listed) shows all processes you can start including **httpd** and mysql**d**. These are also known as **d**aemons (pronounced day-mon, not dee-mon for those who were curious) which are simply background processes running on your server.

For now, let's start our web server with the command:
```
./httpd start
```

You should then see:
```
Starting httpd: [ OK ]
```

Now enable your webserver (httpd) for **ALL future STARTUPS!**

2nd. Edit the config files as applied to the "rc" directory.
Remember that all resource files activated at different run times are in different rc.d directories. When your Linux machine is started it usually loads at runtime level 5. Therefore, all of the resources under the directory named `rc5.d` are activated.

Before you can edit this config file you need to change your directory to:
```
cd /etc/rc.d/rc5.d
```

Remember that the *rc5.d* is a resource directory (under the directory /etc) for run level 5. Run level 4 would be rc4.d and so on.

You **edit** files in these directories to control what occurs at different run levels. Files with a prefix of **K** are NOT installed to run at startup. Files with a prefix of **S** are ready to run at startup. Two file name examples that may be in the directory: `K15httpd   S56xinetd`

In the above example, httpd not installed to run at startup, and the xinetd is installed to run at startup.

You can always use the command:
```
/sbin/chkconfig --add httpd
```
to add the web server to future startups. However, I prefer doing my change manually, as shown below, so I can always control the operation.

3rd. Manually force your webserver to startup using the command:
```
mv K15httpd S15httpd
```

That's it! Your web server process (httpd) is now not only readily available, it will always be loaded at startup! Use the same commands for httpd to get your mysql started by simply using `mysqld` instead.

Step 3. What About Telnet and FTP?

Ok, you're smart enough to have noticed that following the steps above can **not** get telnet or ftp started. That's because **they are not part of the** *initd* **process,** but rather the *xinetd* process. The xinetd process handles the startup of all of your network related protocols etc.

1st. Start telnet first by changing directories to xinetd:
```
cd /etc/xinetd.d/
```

Now you can type **ls** to list all of the processes that can be configured. You'll notice for instance the file `telnet`.

2nd. Edit the telnet file and change two lines:
```
# default: on
...
disabled = no
```

These lines are not adjacent in the file, but usually the first and last lines of the configuration file (in this case *telnet*). You need to **edit all configuration files** that apply to things you're trying to start.

Many processes come by default turned off and disabled = yes. You can edit files like telnet, wu-ftp, etc.

3rd. Force the Automatic Restart

Once you have edited and saved the files with the default line to `on` and the disabled line to `no`, you can force an automatic restart of the `xinetd` to load without rebooting:

/etc/rc.d/init.d/xinetd restart

Finally, you should see:
```
Stopping xinetd: [ OK ] Starting xinetd: [ OK ]
```

That's it! Believe it or not, following all of this you should now have running on your Linux machine a web server (httpd) and telnet!

TIP: Now check to see what processes you have running by using:
```
/sbin/chkconfig -list
```
or just use the long process (ps) command:
```
ps -e | grep http
```

What About MySQL and Wu-FTP?

You can use these **same steps** above to get MySQL and FTP running on your Linux machine. Replace `httpd` with `mysqld`, or replace `telnet` with `wu-ftpd`.

Always remember there is a **difference** between configuration and startup files under initd and xinetd. You edit the configuration files only!

If you run into issues when trying to start up FTP please take a look at the Appendix section named *FTP Doesn't Work (*on page 100) for additional troubleshooting tips and help.

Chapter 14
A Web Server Primer

*This chapter assumes you are using a fully installed version of LINUX with the necessary configuration tools and web server files. Please realize there are examples given that may not exactly match your situation. As always, **think before you do!***

I've included lots of basic tips and ways to avoid traps as you get ready to run a web server of your very own. By the time you finish reviewing this chapter, you will have verified that your server, file system, and network is healthy and ready for serious use!

Check Your Web Server's Health

Okay, before we can go too much further it's always a good idea to see if your web server even has a pulse!

How do you check if *httpd* (the web server process) is even installed?

1. At the prompt type: `locate httpd |more`
OR from a web browser try hitting your localhost with an http:// web call directly to your servers IP such as: `http://10.2.1.1/`

2. Hopefully the above steps verified that your web server has a pulse (aka. Is installed). Now don't forget to verify that your web server is actually running! One simple way to do this is to check for the httpd process. At the prompt type:
`ps -e | grep httpd`

This should tell you right away IF you have the httpd process available. If you do not have this process (ie. if it is not listed) then you need to **get help by going to page 65**! Otherwise, if you see an httpd process listed, you're in fine shape and so, it would seem, is your web server!

Great, now what? Well, usually the next step is to look and see what web pages are active on your server. You can look at your current web server pages by opening any web browser included with Linux. Netscape is always an option on most Linux systems. You can also launch the web browser named Konquerer if you are using the KDE desktop.

Regardless which browser you prefer, open one and begin looking around your web server directories... most likely something like: `/var/www/html`

If you're not sure whether this directory applies to your particular Linux version, then refer to the very first step on page 69 using `locate`. Some of the newer Linux flavors **do not** put a default or dummy index.html page into the web server directories for testing purposes.

Check Your Network's Health

Okay, so let's not forget that before your web server will work well, or you can even think about serving WEB pages, it's necessary to do the network configuration!

I won't try to explain the configuration of your personal network because it is well beyond the scope of this brief introduction. However, as a useful guide and reminder you may want to review the network configuration information from page 13.

Also to help you, here are some of the basics you'll need to keep in mind:
- Use Network Configurator (usually under *Administration* in X) to assign IP addresses as needed. The command is: `netconfig`
- Use LinuxConf (usually under *System* in X) to assign proper rights to your accounts to allow setting up servers etc.
- Check to make sure you have a hostname properly assigned by typing the command: `hostname`

Let's assume your network is properly configured and move on!

Check Your File System's Health

It's important to note the directory that you will use extensively (maybe slightly different based on your Linux flavor): `/var/www/`

The /var/www directory also contains a number of other sub-directories which are used to serve web pages, images, and other items. In fact, you'll find that you spend most of the time in the /var/www directory as you create your website. You might as well go ahead and open several xterm sessions looking at these directories now.

For many of these steps its best to use the `root` login. However, also keep in mind that in the future you should do web server and website maintenance using a *different* login name that you grant access privileges to. Some things like FTP will not even work with a local connection from root login anyway!

Being careful includes taking time to make back-up copies of files you are about to edit. For example:
```
cp filename.ext filename.ext.old
```
(replace filename with the specific file you are copying)

For your convenience and because I also needed a quick table to remind myself where all the webserver directories exist, I've included this table:

Directory	Web Server Use
/var/www/html	Put your web pages like index.html here
/var/www/cgi-bin	Put all CGI related files here like your perl scripts
/var/www/icons	Where your generic web server icons are located
/etc/httpd/logs	Your web server logs are located here

That's it! With this information, and having confirmed the health of your system, you can begin setting up your web site on your very own web server. There are a number of additional tips you may find useful in the Appendix, including a list of Cool Programs for a Web Server beginning on page 102.

If you've gotten this far, I can say with confidence and out of personal experience that you're well on your way to web mastery!

Basic Information Resources
Getting help with webmaster work, especially if you're brand new to it, requires some practice and also good resources for help.

Nothing beats having friends who have personal experience. However, excellent documentation is also available all over the web.

But before you go to the web, a great place to begin (on most Linux versions) is at the dummy index.html page on your own web server.

This dummy index page will provide links and information on further configuration details.

Also, a really helpful web site for beginning web masters is the strangely named but well frequented www.bignosebird.com. This is probably one of the best places to start getting acquainted with web master tips.

Now, for tips on creating CGIs please look over on to the page.

Chapter 15
Web Server Tips for CGI Use

One of the most frequent desires I've heard from new Linux server users is the desire to get CGIs working. After all, once we get our web server running smoothly the next logical step is to create a cool website which often includes CGIs, dynamic pages etc.

I've written this brief chapter in hopes that it will help you quickly address issues and get CGIs working on your new Linux Webserver.

Seven Tips for CGI Newbies

Perhaps you've just downloaded a cool CGI program and are trying to get it working on your Linux Web Server or are simply having trouble with one that you wrote. Here are things I've noticed over the years that tended to resolve almost all of my issues with CGIs on Linux servers.

1. If There's a Readme file Read It!

Carefully and thoroughly read the README that came with your CGI program. Let's face it, you and I will NOT be able to setup most cgi programs on our sites unless we can read this patiently! They often include some hidden nugget of information that is critical for the program to work.

2. Edit CGI Files Carefully

Carefully edit the .cgi file and make sure not to forget to run the **chmod** command as described in the README. If you forgot the settings for chmod, you may want to go back to page 21 and briefly review them.

When editing, please be very careful if you use the PICO editor since it does **not** handle long lines properly and often truncates lines creating errors!

I've spent the better part of a long night at work trying to figure out why in the world a well written perl script kept failing due to this! I recommend using a different text editor if you're doing major edits.

Also, Do NOT change the first line #!/usr/bin/perl unless you know why you're doing so! This first line is critical to the CGI!

3. Fix Bugs In Your CGI File
On more than one occasion I have seen CGI files off the internet that come with some bug or other. One example and very common bug is that somewhere there is a missing close **parenthesis**. Just make sure whenever there's an open **(** there's also a close **)** okay!

4. Test the CGI Perl Script by running the command:
`perl search.cgi`

5. Know the Web Directory Location
Often when the documentation for your CGI refers to your web *root directory* or your www directory, they actually mean the `/home/httpd/` directory which is considered your web root directory. You can always use the *locate httpd* command to find out where on your particular web server this is. In many cases this directory, on your personal Linux server, will be `/var/www/html/`

6. Using tar files?
IF you also happen to be using a TAR file, just note that the tar file may be stupid and cause errors untarring.

Often a tar file when untarred is *suppose* to create a specific directory under your /cgi-bin directory, but for one reason or another does not do so. Instead, you may want to create the correct directory yourself, otherwise you need to be careful to change the directories in the refering .cgi file and form.txt to include the appropriate directory.

Does this 6th tip not make any sense to you? Please ignore it if you're not dealing with a tar file! For help on the `tar` command, see page 29.

7. Always Check the Error_log
The web server error log will have plenty of information if the .cgi is not working properly. Your log files for your web server are usually located under the /etc directory, so try to run the command `locate logs` and see if something like /etc/httpd/logs shows up.

8. It's Probably Something Simple and Silly!
Often CGIs taken off the web tend to be simple installations, so if you're really having problems, stop and check for really simple things!
*(okay, this **8th tip** was a freebee from personal experience!)*

Now You're Ready to Use CGIs!

After placing the appropriate files in the right directories you should be able to insert your form.txt (or other file that uses the perl/CGI) directly into your .html page and see how it works!

If all works smoothly, your server will serve its first dynamic CGI page right before your eyes!

Only Linux allows us to make this happen so quickly and easily from the comfort of our office or home. Yes, I'm gushing a little here because I've made lots of friends as a result of this dramatic ability to concoct web servers and dynamic web sites overnight. I hope you'll enjoy many such successes as well.

Section 4
Stories From the Field

Chapter 16
Linux Can Make You Cool

This section includes stories from the real world and fantasy about the amazing power Linux gives to folks like you and I.

Maybe I should have warned you at the beginning of this book, but getting into Linux, setting up your web server, and tinkering with configurations doesn't just satisfy an insatiable desire we all have to create and achieve, it also makes you cool.

I'm not kidding about this. One of the inevitable results of Linux experience is *coolness*.

About four years ago in the midst of my technical career, I met a gentleman, I'll nickname Earl, who use to make a name solving huge corporate issues. Many knew him, and if they didn't know him they knew *of* him.

I'm not bragging on his behalf here, but this was no small company we were part of.   Today it's called AOL Time Warner. He'd walk into a meeting with me, listen to all the fears and concerns from folks, and then walk out of the room smiling. "I can solve this for them by Thursday afternoon," Earl would tell me as we headed back to our offices.

Now if I hadn't met him, and if at some point I didn't have the blessing of being his technical manager, I would never have believed it. I would have laughed Earl off as a silly fellow with a big mouth.

But Earl was different. Earl was cool. He'd go hide in his office for the night and the next morning he'd pop me an IM asking if I had time to see his latest solution.

The specific issue we were trying to solve at the time was to deliver web site content across all of AOL's multiple brands, using a single publishing tool created with no new resources, that could be learned overnight, and available the "day before yesterday."

No one even thought there was a solution.

Any solution had to be readily available, and capable of running on what we already had. And as the technical manager who inevitably would get voice mails from heated executives, I knew it had to scale.

Earl worked his experience and the *secret formula* into the plan and within a week had a tool delivering pages to the staging servers. When we demo'ed the tool to the important people, one of them stood up and declared, "Now that's cool!"

They couldn't believe that he was able to deliver solutions before executives had time to get worked up.

Well, the "secret" was finally revealed: Linux servers. Few understood that the reason Earl could get so much work done so fast was because he had Linux servers *in his office* enabling him to generate, test, and deliver code faster than some engineers could boot up their workstations.

Yet, on stuff you and I can buy at the corner computer store, Earl was addressing significant corporate infrastructure problems in a matter of weeks, not months, or years. Again and again, he and a number of others on my team did just that.

In incredibly compressed time frames we were able to deliver complete new content tools for editorial staff, substantial new websites that would receive millions of page views, and infrastructure tools to help with managing content and work-flow. All this was possible thanks to their talent, stellar work ethic, and the flexible power Linux servers provided. And of course, the executives who saw it with their own eyes were calling the team "seriously cool."

There are countless more stories and anecdotes from the field on how Linux enables people to do things that simply can not be done in non-open source environments. People like Earl, you, and I are not simply using up time tinkering with Linux, because we have proof that it will make us cool!

Of course, all of this knowledge also leads to being more marketable, better poised to take on new jobs, and exposed to a far wider array of opportunities. But, for now I just enjoy the fact that Linux knowledge makes people cool.

Chapter 17

Even Granny Has Linux

The tips and letters are based on a true to life granny who not only loved Linux, but knew it inside and out. In memory of Granny and because she was a huge fan of Linux, I've included a few "letters."

Hello my dear. I am so thankful you came to learn a little about my favorite Linux programs and for some of my fresh apple pie!

While the pie is cooling, let me introduce you to two programs for Linux I have enjoyed using. These two programs nearly knocked my dentures out!

Want a Great Graphics App? Use Gimp!

GNU's Image Manipulation Program offers so many features usually found in professional desktop applications for the customary Linux price of $0.

Gimp comes preloaded with most versions of Linux. Just install this graphics package when given the option during setup. GIMP is found under *Graphics* in the X-Windows menu. Or just open a command prompt in X-Windows and type: `/usr/bin/gimp`

I'm no artist, but the GIMP allowed me to do some very clever artwork in seconds.

To the right you can see that I have created a pretty sphere with just two clicks of my mouse key and the remarkable Gimp!

There are specialized filters included to customize any graphic you wish. I used the *flare* filter to add a nice touch with one mouse click.

I've also been able to make amazing logos and prints with three simple mouse clicks!

This logo was made in four seconds using Gimp's special Script-Fu tool:

The many features of Script-Fu allow me to create professional looking graphics in under a minute, since all of the complex light and shade calculations are automatically done with the click of a button. Now I'm able to enjoy being creative rather than spending my precious hours sweating and learning.

I'm so thankful for the wonderful folks who helped make the GIMP possible. Thank you Spencer Kimball and Peter Mattis and the other gang of fine folks at Gimp.org. If you were here in my living room I would reach out and hug you all!

Just so you can see the power of GIMP, our well known TUX image (also known as the Linux mascot) created by Larry Ewing was designed in GIMP!

You can find out how Larry did this in Gimp by going to his web page where he also includes some examples to download.

His detailed explanation of how he used Gimp to design and further enhance his image is fun and informative reading.

Go see it at:
www.isc.tamu.edu/~lewing/linux/

Screen Captures in Linux? KSnapshot!

This very handy screen capture tool, by the same folks who bring us the KDE interface, has made capturing images from the video monitor too easy!

Yes, even an old granny can make quality images appear on websites with this tool! If you have Linux installed then you will usually find it under either KDE *Tools* or KDE *Graphics* menu. Or just open a command prompt in X-Windows and type: `/usr/bin/ksnapshot`

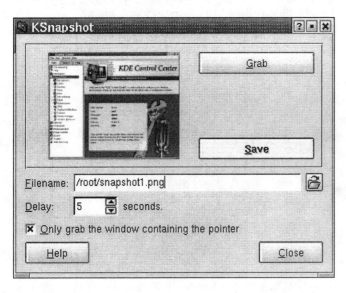

KSnapshot, written by Richard Moore, ensures that even beginners get quality screen shots in Linux without a hitch. All of the screen captures I use for my personal web page graphics and these letters are made using the Ksnapshot tool.

Using both KSnapshot and the GIMP allows even an old grandmother to get real power from Linux and to show it off!

It's been fun! I hope you enjoyed this review of a few of my all time favorite programs available exclusively for Linux at the usual Linux price of $0. God bless you! Have a real nice day and don't forget to put on a sweater so you don't catch cold!

Love,
Granny

P.S. Don't Forget MultiMedia!

I'm sorry to be rambling, but I can't contain my excitement. Just today I began using my wonderful Linux X Multi Media System (XMMS). This tool comes with most flavors of Linux, so just open a command prompt in X-Windows and type: `/usr/bin/xmms`

This tool allows me to rock back in my chair, sip tea, and enjoy listening to favorite tunes on the PC.

The XMMS interface is beautifully easy to look at and use. Those dear people at 4front Technologies, like Peter Alan, and others, have made my day with music!

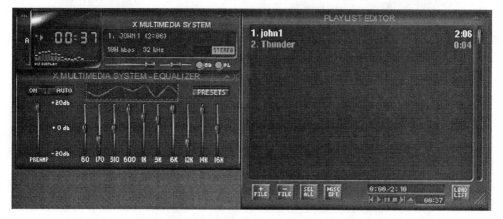

If you try this tool, be sure to change the *theme* in your desktop to get the most beautiful version of the interface! You can do so using the command `switchdesk` on most Linux versions.

XMMS comes with many features and options to allow me hours of enjoyment listening to my favorite tunes, whether from a CD or wav files my grandkids email me.

How amazing it is that Linux came with so many free tools already preloaded. As I peak over at my menu, there must be at least seventy free programs, from calculators, to personal information managers, to PDA tools, and of course XMMS! Where else can I get so much for free? I feel like its Christmas!

Oh dear, Sorry I've kept you so long... I've gotta go. It's time to play a few rounds of chess against my Linux system!

Chapter 18
Granny Dumps MSOffice for StarOffice on Linux

In this brief letter Granny tells how she easily switched from MS-Office to the fully compatible StarOffice, gaining the benefits of Linux.

Hello my dear,
I am so thankful you came to learn a little about my favorite Linux programs and for some of my home made apple cider! While the cider is cooling, let me introduce you to the amazing **StarOffice** software.

I went from using Microsoft Office to the fully compatible and easy to use SUN StarOffice on my stable and inexpensive Linux computer.

It is such a joy to gain both the stability of Linux and the compatibility needed to exchange files with my dear grandchildren. I was so concerned that moving to Linux would mean I was no longer able to be compatible and exchange files with others. Within moments after installing StarOffice, I realized this was not true at all and that I had been tricked!

Instead, I found that I could easily edit my MS Word .doc files, make changes to old PowerPoint .ppt files, and even update an Excel .xls spreadsheet all from the convenience of StarOffice for Linux!

I've included a screen capture of me opening a .ppt file in Linux that my grandkids emailed me.

I could edit and save to the file formats I knew most people used, without sacrificing stability, or my hard earned money!

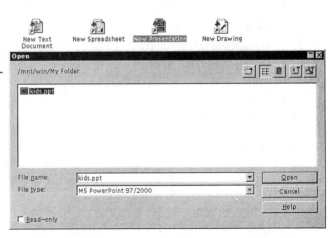

How easy the StarOffice creators made it for me to switch. The menus and features were so simple and similar that I could begin using StarOffice immediately. Below I have a screen capture of the StarOffice main menu, which is a breeze to use if you are familiar with other tools.

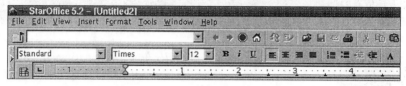

This shows how even an old lady like me can easily make this change from Microsoft Office to StarOffice! Most important of all, I don't have to waste my meager retirement money on the expensive Office software, when I can get StarOffice for so much cheaper.

But please don't take my word for it. I want you to see for yourself that making the switch away from Microsoft is easy and still totally compatible! I've included the website to the fully operational OpenOffice program, which is the free open source version:
http://www.openoffice.org/dev_docs/source/1.0.1/index.html

It may be free but it is also totally compatible with the latest file formats like the ones below:

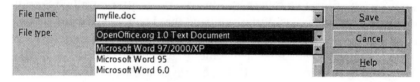

You can buy the StarOffice package at your favorite computer software store or go directly to the SUN website!

I'm very thankful you let me share this great news with you since I know you'll love the power of your Linux StarOffice!

With love,
Granny

Chapter 19
Gus Talks Tough On Linux

Gus is a man of many words, and in this candid interview he hasn't changed his tone or verboseness.

I approached Gus in his favorite "thinking" place, Really Deep Creek Lake, to ask him where his thoughts are on Linux.

Mark: Gus what is your take on the explosive and unique Linux phenomenon?

Gus: Phooey! That's right, it's Phooey! That guy from Microsoft put it good when he sat up at the shareholders meeting and said something about it being for small fry ISPs.

Mark: Ok. Then how do you see the latest reports about Linux growing into a significant share of the OS Server market?

Gus: Frankly that's hogwash. It's about as slimy a number as this here dead fish I'm holding. [*holds up a rancid fish in his hand*] Truth is that Microsoft still kicks behind in the server market, and although Microsoft servers are a boat load more expensive, they get the job done well.

Mark: Do you see Linux's relatively low price as a reason for its success in penetrating the server market?

Gus: You startin' to give me the willies! NO way is Linux succeeding, because it is what it is — cheap! You get what you pay for and in my case I much prefer paying the cost of Microsoft Back Office Server for several thousand dollars.

I saw one of those Linux Professional versions for something crazy like a hundred fifty bucks! I'm guessing I'm going to get what I pay for and if I pay almost nothing, I am going to get as much.

Mark: Well Gus, how do you account for the large and growing market share of Linux?

Gus: Marketing! Them marketers of Linux are using big money and hype to push this on to poor defenseless folks who don't know better. After all, think about it this way, Microsoft is a name I know and I'm willing to pay a lot for that name.

Mark: I'm curious how you decipher this since Linux is not a product owned by a specific company? What are your thoughts about the latest benchmark test showing Linux servers compete head to head?

Gus: You keep talking like that and I'm going to slap this fish up side your head! *[makes an aggressive gesture with the dead fish he's still holding]* Now let's stop blabbering about Linux and get fishing!

Now that's one big fish!

6' 340 lbs Tuna
North Atlantic

Chapter 20
Small Company Saves Big Using Linux

 Joe runs a small business that needed infrastructure at minimal cost.

This brief interview sheds some light on the reality so many SOHO's face when given the option to buy PCs that are cheaper than the software suites they run.

Mark: Joe, give us some insight how you changed gears with your business and moved to use Linux exclusively?

Joe: We saw some great priced PCs at the local retailer – I mean really great priced PCs -- and purchased ten systems. These were solid machines, all Pentium systems with plenty of RAM.

Mark: So, what happened next?

Joe: Our system administrator, Michael, was in charge of setting up and getting them ready for our new employees. A few days later I had a note from Michael with a check request for over $4200 -- for software! We only spent about $3000 on all ten systems!

Mark: What were you planning on doing with the systems?

Joe: That's where it gets even more frustrating. It seemed ridiculous to me that we would need to pay more for software, in this case Office Pro, just so my staff could be typing letters, printing documents, managing basic spreadsheets, or making a few presentation slides. It was disturbing and discouraging to me. We didn't have extra money to be throwing around.

Mark: Microsoft offers bulk prices for licensing. Did you look into prices and options?

Joe: Yes, we talked through all of the options. The best price we negotiated for the MS Office licenses was still more than all of the hardware.

Mark: What about other software? Perhaps a simplified suite like MS Works?

Joe: It couldn't do the job. Everyone kept reminding me that the rest of the world worked in Office and we would need to be able to exchange data, like emailing power point slides.

Mark: So, is this when you went with Linux?

Joe: Honestly, no. I didn't considered Linux as a viable option, since we wanted to be compatible with the rest of the world. However, shortly afterwards, I met a friend with Linux installed. He showed me how his Linux included SUN's StarOffice suite that allowed compatibility to MS Office programs.

Mark: Is this when you moved to buy Linux?

Joe: Indeed, yes! For just thirty-nine dollars I saw a stable operating system like Microsoft's, with all of the tools we needed to get the job done, AND while remaining compatible with the rest of the world.

Mark: What was the key factor that sold you to move your business to Linux?

Joe: The factor that sold me was the fact that Linux allowed me to do all the same things for far less cost.

Mark: If you had a chance to talk to business owners in the same situation, what are some thoughts you would convey?

Joe: It seems we have reached a time when the PCs are less expensive than the software they run. This is a big barrier to entry for small businesses until they consider Linux. The initial concerns we had were quickly addressed once we began using Linux.

Chapter 21
Linux Revolution

A *Tale* of Two Men and a Machine

We had waited until midnight before starting to install Linux.

With all of the lights off, we dimmed the monitor so that it's hue would not reflect out of the windows. The phone lay off the hook, and Peter kept peaking through the blinds out onto the dark parking lot.

Were we being paranoid? When everyone is after you, you've got to be.

I slipped the CD into the drive and let the installation begin. It didn't take long before the graphical icons appeared and walked me through each step of getting Linux started on the machine. We heard foot steps, then some muffled shouts from above us. It was the renter upstairs. He and his wife bought a new PC for the holidays and then started quarreling -- making a general nuisance of themselves.

The footsteps subsided and I figured it was another of their typical "what did you do to the computer" followed by "I didn't touch it, it just screwed up and gave that blue screen with the fatal error thingy!" Peter and I exchanged nods; another marriage tearing apart under the strain of an operating system.

Five minutes and we were finished. The old operating system had been wiped clean and replaced with Linux. I rebooted and watched as X Windows began. Double clicking on the OpenOffice icon, I laughed in joy as the word processor and spreadsheet programs appeared.

"Free! Bloody free!" Peter yelled gleefully. It had cost us nothing but a few hours of downloading Linux and the associated software to cleanse the machine and restart it with Linux and a host of other goods.

"Shut your traps you yanks!" screamed a voice through the ceiling as the renter upstairs reacted to our mini-celebration.

In our bliss we stopped paying attention to the front entrance or the parking lot. A loud knock was quickly followed by another at the door.

Peter jumped out of his seat. I sat back calmly in my chair waiting.

Suddenly, the front door was rammed open and folks from the yard paid us a visit. Searching frantically, they approached the computer. A rather burly gentlemen yanked me back by my shoulders.

One of the men from Scotland Yard started playing with the mouse and clicking icons. He typed, clicked a few times, then typed again.

"There's not a bloody piece of unlicensed software or illegally possessed program here!" he blurted in frustration.

The other men, opening up my cd cases and tenaciously searching for software, also knew the truth. In disgust they threw the CDs to the floor and left our pad grumbling. Peter wiped his sweaty brow and smiled.

Two gents at midnight had played a role in the operating system revolution. You don't need to buy, barter or steal Linux – it's free!

Chapter 22

Linux At Its Best

The Inside Story of a Man, a Machine, and a Migraine

I was hunched over my computer, kindly given to me for free by my friend Bob. He encouraged me to try out home networking and I appreciated his generosity.

My first task was to install my unused license of an older Windows OS onto the PC. Yes, I admit it. I was trying to avoid paying $'s for a new OS on this *free* PC. I booted the system and started it up. An error message appeared... something silly about my network connection being misconfigured.

The whole point of having an extra machine was to gain some performance and be able to learn more about home networking.

Here I was, four hours later, still trying to get the Windows network drivers to work properly. I screamed out in agony, took a breath, and then called my buddy Bob.

"You trying to install a simple network? No biggie, upgrade to the next Windows. That'll do it," Bob said before hanging up.

So, I headed to the nearest store, plopped my charge card down and purchased an upgrade for Windows, supposedly with all of the network drivers and things I'd need.

It was around 9pm. I had goofed with what should have been a "simple thing" for six hours and was starting to get a bad headache and neck cramp. Applying pressure to the side of my aching head, I tapped the keyboard and watched as Windows slowly installed.

I don't like to complain, but it took five minutes to get from the logo screen to the place I could do something. Everything else I did from that point was even slower.

My left eye began to twitch, and I could literally feel the blood vessels on the side of my head throbbing, as I called Bob again.

"Oh, gotcha. Yeah, what you really need is Windows98, it runs better on an older machine like yours. I had bought a copy a long time ago for my other PC which I don't use, you're welcome to try."

So, around 10:15pm I drove over to Bob and got his unused Windows CD. The installation was about the same, but as Bob promised, load up was faster.

Now, finally I could get my network operational and get the two machines to talk to each other. The older machine was also using a license of Windows98, which it came with, so I tinkered with both machines' configurations and drivers. I kept using every technique I knew to get the two talking. I tried ping, assigning new IP addresses, even changing protocols from IPX to TCP back and forth ... but nothing!

My left eye stopped twitching. The eyelid just sort of drooped, and as I clutched my head, a clump of hair came out in my hand. I felt nauseous, probably because of the headache, so I grabbed several pain relievers and chewed them like candy.

I stared at the monitor. The operating system was kind enough to display the clock at the lower right hand. It was 11:45pm. Almost nine hours of installing, reinstalling, tinkering with Windows setting this and Windows setting that, and nothing!

"This is insane," I yelled at the top of my lungs as I threw my Windows manual across the room into a pile of CD cases!!!

By now you may think I'm some kind of illiterate when it comes to PCs. I don't consider myself an expert, but the basics of networking and system installation I can do... or could do.

What now? Call Bob? It's almost midnight. Well -- it was Bob who started this whole mess with his stupid suggestion! So I picked up the phone and what do you know, he answered!

"Nothing? Maybe it's because you're using an old pc with an old Windows. Did you try upgrading both systems?" Bob said.

Now don't get me wrong, I like Bob, but this "upgrading" remark at 11:50pm after nine hours, and a throbbing migraine, was enough to break any man.

"Upgrade my foot," I yelled into the phone!

Bob, being the rather patient type, just replied, "sorry man the only thing I can suggest is to upgrade the other PC or upgrade your hardware to be more compatible."

I thanked him for his information and letting me call so late. It really was late and the day had been wasted. Clasping my head in disbelief I looked on the floor at the pile of scattered CDs. Out of the corner of my eye I saw a CD case that had been snapped open by the manual I threw. It was a Linux CD that I had borrowed and procrastinated in returning. I decided to plunk it into the PC and with the last bit of energy I had, to run the install process.

Then, I got to the prompt and X Windows loaded. I closed a number of windows and slid my mouse over the xterm icon. My heart started racing and my head stopped throbbing.

I typed very deliberately, ping 10.1.1.2, the IP of the other PC. *Packet confirmed*! I jumped over to the old pc and ran an ancient version of telnet. Instantly, I was looking at the Server login prompt! I was in!

It was 12:55am and I had a fully operational network, a web server, and it flew! On this free PC I was running several simultaneous logins, playing the worm game, and writing this article! My X Windows session started in less than ten seconds, and I began to whistle tunes as I typed away.

It took over ten hours, a lot of pain, and probably a lot of broken friendships - Bob doesn't speak to me much anymore and my roommates were wondering if I didn't want to look for a nicer place - but I had learned my lesson.

Sitting in the dark room and glow of my monitor at 1am, I finally understood Linux at its best... **free, flexible, and fast.**

###

Section 5
Appendix

Appendix
Some Questions and Answers

Over the past few years I've received a number of questions from folks just start-ing out with Linux. I've included some of the ones people asked me the most of-ten here in this brief section.

 ## Installation Tips & Tricks

What Do I Do If My Linux CD Doesn't Boot?
I've heard of a number of people who are trying to install the latest Linux on their older PCs. Often the issue then becomes how to get the Linux CD to boot-up for installation.

The simple answer is that if your system's BIOS does not allow boot-up off of the Linux CD-ROM or if your existing Operating System does not allow this, you'll need to create a boot diskette and use the diskette to do the initial boot up. The steps for doing this are described on page 31.

Unrecognized Video Adapter?!
A handful of people have contacted me as they were in the middle of their Linux installation and got into the step where the video installation attempts to 'probe' for a video card. Either the installation simply can not find a video adapter it recognizes, or it fails all together. In some cases the installation confuses things even more by asking for video chip sets etc.

First of all, I'm sorry you encountered this! I've been through this many times and there are a number of options to deal with the issue.

- One way to avoid this issue is to use the *generic* video card setup.
- Another way is to upgrade the Linux version if you are using an very old release. Newer Linux releases contain many more video drivers.
- Finally, you can make an adjustment in your computer's BIOS. Usually this is done by pressing the Del key or F2 keys when starting your system. In the BIOS menu, under Plug-and-Play menu option, change the setting so it does not say Plug-n-Play by OS or Operating System. The options are usu-ally Windows OS or Hardware. Choosing *Hardware* (or *System*) and then retrying your installation may solve the issue.

Linux does not need the Plug-n-play forced to an OS, and in fact installing Linux with your BIOS set to Windows OS may cause install problems like yours. For more details turn to page 47 which refers to X-Windows video selection.

How to Install SUN StarOffice On Linux?
Even if your Linux release comes with the excellent Sun StarOffice package, it often doesn't get preinstalled with your Linux OS. For example, most Red Hat users have this included on a separate CD named *workstation*.

In almost all cases you can simply insert the CD-ROM that includes this package and browse under the "StarOffice" directory. There you should find a file named something similar to "run.rmp" or a file with the word "installation" in its name. Simply double click on this file to begin installation of StarOffice.

IF you can not find the .rmp file or other installation file on your CD-ROM it may be that you're using a different Linux flavor or one that didn't come with this software in the first place.

You can directly download the free version from the SUN web site: http://www.openoffice.org/dev_docs/source/1.0.1/index.html, or you can purchase the SUN StarOffice software for a very reasonable price.

FTP Doesn't Work On the Server?!
If your Linux system seems operable, with network configuration working, but your FTP doesn't work, you may have a simple configuration issue.

This is very often the case if you get the error:
`"421 Service not available, remote server has closed connection."`

Before you look at the troubleshooting steps below, please ensure that you've followed the directions from page 66 on configuring your FTP server.

1. CHECK YOUR /etc/hosts.allow
The most common reason for an error is missing information in this file. Check your actual host permissions, since 'localhost' and the localhost IP and user may simply not be given permissions! This is especially the case if others can login, but your local host cannot. For example, I added the line below (which is my host IP) to the hosts.allow file using a text editor:
`10.2.1.1`
(By the way, I always suggest using a different login than 'root' for using FTP!)

In some instances the error instead comes from other files or directories that have the **wrong permissions**. One of several ways to fix this is to lookup in the hosts file and see where it points to DNS -- where it is actually defined, and make necessary chmod permissions changes if needed. This may not be necessary in your case. If you're not familiar with chmod or file permissions then take a quick peak at page 21.

2. CHECK SHELL ACCESS
Please check your /etc/shells which needs the correct access rights (world readable and not world writable) for users to use ftp on your server.

3. CHECK XINETD CONFIGURATION
Edit /etc/xinetd.d/wu-ftp and make sure it has been "enabled" properly.

4. CHECK YOUR SERVER LOGS
You definitely check your server logs to see if any more details about the error with FTP are showing up there. Most error logs will be located under your /etc/httpd/logs directory or simply use the command:
```
locate logs ¦ more
```
and visually look for the location of your error log files.

 # Getting Started with a WEB Server

Where Are My Web Server Files?
This is by far one of the top questions I get from beginning Linux users who just finished installing their server. The essence of the question really has to do with where you put the actual files that you want seen by users. It's a very good question that is easily answered for *most* Linux versions.

The website files on most servers are located under the directory:
/var/www/

Your html files like index.html simply go under the directory:
/var/www/html

For cgi-bin files (perl scripts etc.) you would look under:
/var/www/cgi-bin

For MP3's (or other music files), it's a matter of creating a directory under /var/www/html named mp3 and placing files there. These files will then be available from your web pages such as index.html.

Of course as you get started using your Web Server, also keep in mind:

1. You must ensure your server's network is configured or you won't get access to your server domain name.

You can do this by typing the command: `netconfig`

2. You will need to make sure your httpd (web server daemon) is running properly. Refer to the details on page 63 for Configuring a Linux Server.

 Cool Programs for My Web Server

Over the last few years, I've had lots of excited people run into my office or email me with glee that they have a web server running. But their excitement dies down and they suddenly ask "now what?"

Well, being one who never wants the excitement for Linux to die down, of course I have some suggestions! For those ready to put their new web server to real use as an intranet server or a great learning tool, I recommend checking out a few programs that I use myself and have greatly benefited from.

I know there are countless other very good programs out there as well. I include these three that I use every day on my web server to run my web site. I can't officially endorse any specific product, but list at least these three examples as a basic review of what you can do with your web server.

What's a good free Web Site Search Engine?
Focal Media.Net   www.focalmedia.net
This is an easy to install site search with ultra fast results! It took me 15 minutes to setup and run on my servers. I love having this on my website because it is maintenance free, absolutely flies with small content web sites, does a full text search, and is free!

The only drawback I've had from experience is that once your site expands to greater than several hundred pages this search bogs down brutally under its full text constraint. Also the algorithm to calculate relevance ranking is somewhat limited.

How can I easily add a Web Message Board System?
Ikonboard.com   www.ikonboard.com
My mother could install and run this message board system on my Linux servers, it is that simple to install and use. It comes with an administrator interface where adding board members, creating news events, and even making chat available are just button clicks away.

On the down side, this program is no longer offered as free software, but requires a minimal fee to purchase for use on your site.

Are there any simple to install Automated Web Publishing tools?
Post-Nuke.com   www.postnuke.com
There is no faster, easier way to setup a complete automated web site than with
the FREE Postnuke web content management system. You'll be amazed not
only how thorough this tool is for web site publishing and content management,
but also how much work has been done. There is a volunteer army of out-
standing Linux engineers and designers constantly adding features and enhance-
ments.

One of only a few cons I see with this tool is its uncanny restriction of web site
design. Very complex designs simply break the modularized mold and can not
be done using this tool.

 # General Linux Questions

Help, the error "`File is not readable`" keeps showing up?!
This error will often show up when you are trying to configure your server or
work on files that require super user access.

One quick solution is to login to your Linux system as root. The other is to type
`su` (for super user) at the prompt and then enter your root password.

In both cases, you will gain super user privileges which should end this error
from appearing.

How Can I Control My Server Remotely?
There are a number of options. However, one solution that is available with
most flavors of Linux is the tool called **Webmin**. This handy application allows
you to monitor all Linux services remotely. It is a very simple interface to your
Linux server and offers useful features that allow you to manage: users, disk
quotas, telnet connections, and CRON jobs.

There are some security implications if you plan to use webmin for servers in a
corporate environment! Be sure you keep this in mind.

The tool can be hosted either on the secure (https) or the standard (http) protocols, and can be found on port `10000` of your web server.
For example, type: `http://<yourhostname/iphere>:10000/`

Replace the <yourhostname/iphere> with **either** your server's hostname or your
system's IP address. Also please don't include the < or > since they are part of
the *example* only.

This should bring up a prompt asking you for a username and password. Enter your root login information to get full access.

If your version did not include this tool or you want the latest version, then download the tool at the web site: www.webmin.com

How Do I Avoid Retyping LONG Commands?
Here are two solutions to avoid retyping extra long commands:

1. You can use the ! at the shell prompt. By pressing the ! followed by the first letter of your command you avoid retyping the entire thing!

2. To avoid retyping a common but long command create a command file. I was tired retyping the lengthy command to mount my windows drive:
mount -t vfat /dev/hda1 /mnt/win
(note: I had already created the /mnt/win directory)

So being the type that prefers short cuts, I just did this:
- Created a file by typing: pico mountnow
- Edited the new file by simply typing in the long mount command on the first line of the file and then saving the file
- Made the file executable: chmod 766 mount
- Then ran the command by simply typing: bash mountnow

Total Index

For clarity all errors are in italics and all commands are in lower case.